D0700114

The Deer Hunter's Illustrated Dictionary

Other Books by Dr. Leonard Lee Rue III

The Deer of North America

The Deer Hunter's Encyclopedia

How I Photograph Wildlife and Nature

How to Photograph Animals in the Wild

The World of the White-Tailed Deer

Leonard Lee Rue III's Whitetails

Leonard Lee Rue III's Way of the Whitetail

Furbearing Animals of North America

Meet the Beaver

The World of the Raccoon

Cottontail Rabbit

Pictorial Guide to the Mammals of North America

New Jersey Out-of-Doors

The Deer Hunter's Illustrated Dictionary

Full Explanations of More Than 600 Terms and
Phrases Used by Deer Hunters Past and Present

Dr. Leonard Lee Rue III

The Lyons Press
Guilford, Connecticut
An imprint of The Globe Pequot Press

This book is dedicated with love to my nieces and nephews:

Lester Lee Rowe
James Edward Rowe
Robert John Rowe
Ronald Jay Rowe
Joan Kinney
Doris Kinney Richter
Nancy Kinney Fleming
Kathy Guthrie Merzena
Kristin Lee Guthrie
Tom Arthur Rue
Amy Elizabeth Rue

Copyright © 2001 by Dr. Leonard Lee Rue III

All photos © Leonard Lee Rue III unless otherwise indicated

All rights reserved. No part of this book may be reproduced or transmitted in any form by any means, electronic or mechanical, including photocopying and recording, or by any information storage and retrieval system, except as may be expressly permitted by the 1976 Copyright Act or in writing from the publisher. Requests for permission should be addressed to The Globe Pequot Press, P.O. Box 480, Guilford, CT 06437.

Printed in the United States of America

10 9 8 7 6 5 4 3 2 1

Library of Congress Cataloging-in-Publication Data

Rue, Leonard Lee.
    The deer hunter's illustrated dictionary : full explanations of more than 600 terms and phrases used by deer hunters past and present / Leonard Lee Rue III.
        p. cm.
    ISBN 1-58574-349-6
    1. Deer hunting—Dictionaries. I. Title.

SK301 .R85 2001
799.2'765'03—dc21
                                                                2001050271

Contents

Acknowledgments

I am indebted to everyone who has written the thousands upon thousands of books I've read. I have over 16,000 reference books in my library; I sit here surrounded by walls of books. I am indebted to the writers of the tens of thousands of magazine and newspaper articles I have read and of the thousands I have clipped and filed. So much information in an article never gets into a book. I am indebted to my family, as I was brought up in a world of books. This is my 29th book, and I have co-authored seven others. I have written over 1,200 magazine and newspaper articles and columns and given over 4,000 lectures and seminars. I have tried to give back to others the information I have received and learned. Every time I learn something new, I have to write about it; I have to share it with everyone.

I want to thank Jay Cassell, my editor, for proposing that I write this book. I've really enjoyed the writing of it. My thanks to Marilyn Maring, my secretary, for deciphering what I write longhand and for helping me keep my tenses straight. I think a lot faster than I can write and at times that catches up with me. My thanks to my son, Leonard Lee Rue IV (Len Rue Jr.), who provided some of the photos used herein. My special thanks to my dear wife, Uschi, who helps and supports me in all that I do.

God be with all of you,
Leonard Lee Rue III

Introduction

I love words.

I actually enjoy reading a dictionary. As an author and a lecturer, I work with words all the time. I often tell young people that words are one of the most powerful forces in the world. Without words you can't even think. An idea is nothing if you can't communicate it to others, and you can't communicate your ideas to others without words.

I love the nuances, the precise meaning, the shading and gradations that you can impart by using the proper words, but that's not what this book is about. This book attempts to define the words that hunters, and others, need to know to better understand the deer and their world.

In reading sporting magazines and watching outdoor television shows and videotapes, folks are going to hear or see words used that they may not use themselves or may not understand. That's nothing to be ashamed of, because all of us, especially me, are learning new words all the time. My home is full of dictionaries; I have them in every room in the house. I have a number of the most comprehensive collegiate and professional dictionaries I could find. I have biological, zoological, and scientific dictionaries, and none of them have all of the words I need to know, but I'm trying. I copy all of the glossaries I can get my hands on. I'm writing this book to help you get more out of what you see and hear.

Why do you need to know all these words? Actually, you don't need to know all of these words, but the more words you know, the better hunter you will be. As research on cervids is constantly in progress, new information about the deer family and their habits continues to come to light. And that could, or should, make you a better hunter.

When my editor, Jay Cassell, suggested I do a dictionary of words and terms about deer and deer hunting, I jumped at the chance. When I say "deer" here, I am talking about deer, elk, caribou, and moose, all members of the deer family, the Cervidae.

Actually, if I can just get all hunters to refer to the antlers on deer, elk, caribou, and moose as antlers instead of calling them horns, I will feel that we are making progress.

The Deer Hunter's Illustrated Dictionary

A

Aberrant behavior

Whenever a creature does anything that is not considered normal, it is called aberrant behavior. Although it is most unusual, several times each year we get reports of a wild white-tailed buck attacking a human being.

Abomasum

All of the ruminants have a four-chambered stomach. The abomasum is the fourth compartment and is actually the "true stomach" of the deer. In adult deer, the fibrous food goes directly into the rumen, then is regurgitated, re-chewed, re-swallowed, and then passed into the reticulum, the omasum, and into the abomasum, where gastric juices help digest

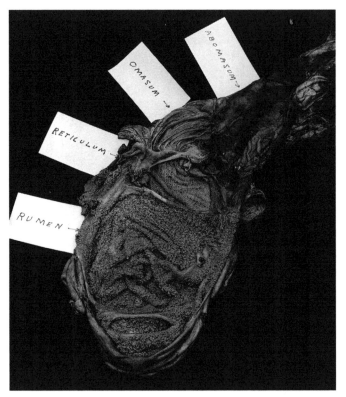

The four compartments of a deer's stomach.

the food before it passes into the small intestine. In fawns, the milk they drink goes along an esophageal groove, bypassing the rumen, reticulum, and omasum, and goes directly into the abomasum.

Adaptive behavioral strategies

These are strategies that the creatures have adapted, not done by instinct, in order to survive. Originally, deer fed more in the daytime, but hunting pressure forced them to feed more at dawn and dusk when human activities are less. Big, trophy deer move only under the cover of darkness, even during the rut, because they have learned that their chances of survival are much better if they do so.

Adrenaline

Adrenaline is a hormone, produced by the adrenal glands, that enters the bloodstream during times of stress. The hormone causes the deer to be more alert, increases its heartbeat, increases its oxygen intake, slows down digestion, and readies the animal for "flight or fight." It is the adrenaline in a deer's system that allows it to run a hundred yards or more following a shot through the heart.

Adrenaline also toughens meat. The meat of a deer that is relaxed when shot will be more tender than the meat of one that has adrenaline in its system when shot.

Aerial census

To get a more accurate count on their game animal populations, many state game departments will take an aerial census using a helicopter or a slow-flying fixed-wing aircraft. The census is usually run in winter when all of the leaves are off the trees and there is snow on the ground. Even so, it is very difficult to detect deer that are bedded down in an evergreen yarding area. When running a census in such areas, the biologists use infrared film or heat-seeking devices. Although the aerial census is the easiest and the best method available,

A mule deer herd photographed from the air.

many game departments can't afford to do it because of the high cost of using helicopters and airplanes.

Aerial transects

In taking an aerial survey, the plane is not flown randomly. The area to be censused is plotted out on a map in a grid fashion, and then transects, predetermined parts of the grid, are flown. At times, absolute straight lines are flown; at other times, overlapping circles will be flown. Usually the plane flies at a set altitude and the spotters count only the animals seen at a designated distance on their respective side of the plane.

Afterbirth

After the deer fawn, or the elk, caribou, or moose calf, has been born, the placental sac in which the fetus developed and was nourished when in the mother's uterus is passed out. Sometimes the mother will help rid her body of this "afterbirth" by pulling it from her vagina with her teeth. The mother usually eats the afterbirth to prevent its odor from attracting predators. By eating the afterbirth, the mother also returns some of the nutrients to her own body. It is thought that eating the afterbirth also stimulates the production of the colostrum milk.

Aggression

Unlike human aggression, which is usually the result of a calculated move, aggression in members of the deer family is usually in response to hormonal influence. We are all aware of the aggression between the males of the different species

The aggressive posture of a white-tailed buck.

during the rutting season. Sometimes this aggression is even directed against humans. Testosterone is usually the steroid responsible for this type of aggression.

A cow moose protecting her calf displays extreme aggression and, in my opinion, is as dangerous as a grizzly sow protecting her cubs. Epinephrine produced by the adrenal glands is the cause of this aggression.

Aging by the teeth

Jack Tanck and C. W. Severinghaus developed the system of aging deer by the wear on their teeth. Basically, there is 10 mm of first molar tooth sticking up above the gum line,

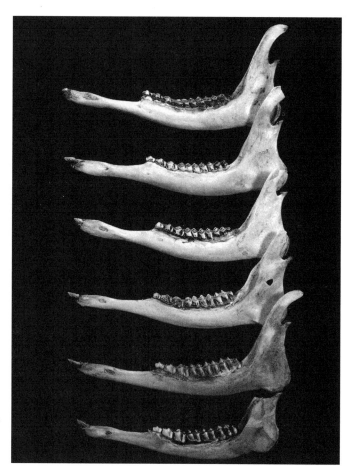

From top to bottom, the jawbone and teeth are from white-tailed deer aged 1½, 2½, 3½, 5½, 7½, and 9½ years old.

measured from the gum line to the buccal crest, when the deer is 1½ years old. Under normal conditions, the teeth wear down about 1 mm a year. In areas where there is sandy soil, such as southern New Jersey, the teeth wear down a little faster because the frequent wind coats the leaves of the vegetation with sandy particles. The particles, being exceptionally hard, cause the teeth to wear down faster because of increased abrasion. This is the most accurate method of aging deer that can be accomplished by any hunter in the field.

A much more accurate method has been developed by biologists, but this can only be performed in a laboratory. One of the deer's incisor teeth is pulled. The tooth is decalcified to soften it. It is then sliced longitudinally, and, after staining, the layers of cementum are counted as one would count the growth rings on a tree. See *cementum.*

Aging meat

To age meat properly, it must be kept at a temperature between 34 degrees F° to 38 degrees F°. At colder temperatures the meat freezes and all bacteria action stops; warmer than that temperature range and the bacteria action speeds up and may cause the meat to spoil. As most of us do not have access to a walk-in refrigerator, I allow my deer carcass to hang overnight to remove all body heat and then butcher early the next morning. You can age the butchered meat in your refrigerator at the above temperatures for four to five days, which will help tenderize the meat.

Agonistic behavior

This is aggressive behavior carried to the extent that it is a threat of an imminent fight. This is when the rival bucks, or bulls, are no longer bluffing, but have put it all on the line.

Alarm bark

This is a high-pitched, short, nasal sound that cow elk give when they are suspicious of something and they want to warn the herd. It is a call that they also give when they are searching for a calf that may have strayed out of sight. Ordinarily, a cow elk and her calf stay close to each other all the time, but during the rutting season, when the cows are being herded by the dominant bull and rival bulls are attempting to cut some of the cows, chaos is the order of the day. They may get separated, and the cow may then give the alarm bark so her calf can locate her again.

Alarm calls

All members of the deer family pay close attention to every alarm call made by crows, jays, ravens, squirrels, chipmunks, beaver tail slaps, and so on. There is a saying, "The night has a thousand eyes." Well, so does the forest. For every creature we see, at least a hundred see us and either stay hidden, sneak off, or sound an alarm call. If we are discovered by any of the creatures, we are discovered by all.

Alarm posture

You can ordinarily gauge how alarmed a deer or an elk is by how high it holds its head. Caribou and moose do this less often. The more intense the alarm, the higher the head is held, and both ears are angled forward. The entire body is tensed. Caribou extend a hind leg backward. In white-tailed deer, this position usually includes the raising and flaring of the tail. The intensity of the pose is instantly recognized by every animal in the herd as they, too, shift into instant alert even though they may not be sure what it was that alerted the first animal.

Alaskan barren ground caribou (*Rangifer tarandus granti*)

These are the largest-antlered of the five subspecies of caribou that are recognized by taxonomists today. The animals range across Alaska and the northwestern portion of the Yukon Territory. There are 22 recognized herds of caribou in Alaska. At the time this is written, most of the herds are increasing in number, while others, such as the McKinley herd, have greatly de-

The more alert a deer is, the higher it holds its head. Credit: Irene Vandermolen

Alaskan barren ground caribou bull in velvet. Credit: Len Rue, Jr.

creased. The number one Boone & Crockett head scored 465⅛ points and was taken by Roger Hedgecock on Mosquito Creek, Alaska, in 1987.

Alaskan-Yukon moose (*Alces alces gigas*)

As the *gigas* in the name implies, the Alaskan-Yukon moose is the largest of the four species; it is gigantic. It is the largest member of the deer family in the world. Big bulls stand over seven feet high at the shoulder and weigh over 1,600 pounds. I have seen some of these big bulls with antlers that had at least a 72-inch spread. The 49ᵗʰ ranked B&C head had an 80⅝-

Huge Alaskan bull moose—a trophy to make any hunter proud.
Credit: Len Rue Jr.

inch spread. The current world record scored 261⅝ points. Although it only had a 65⅛-inch spread, it had both mass and 34 points. It was shot by John Crouse on the Forty Mile River in Alaska in 1994.

Albino

Albinism is caused by recessive genes. Where both parents carry and pass on these characteristics, their offspring do not produce the pigments needed to have the proper color. A true albino in the deer family will have white hair, pink eyes, and gray hooves. The pink eyes are not the result of color but occur because the blood in the eye vessels can be seen. True albinos often have a hearing deficiency. They are frequently shunned by the other animals in the herd.

Alces

Alces, the Latin species name given to the European moose, means elk. In Europe today, their moose is still called an elk. When the first settlers came to the North American continent, they mistakenly called our native elk, wapiti by the Indian name, an elk. However, *Alces* had previously been assigned, scientifically, to the European moose, so our American moose are also classified as *Alces.* Within the species, different subspecies are further identified with a Latin subspecies name, such as *alces americana, alces andersoni,* and *alces gigas.*

Alfalfa

Alfalfa is a legume that has the ability to trap nitrogen from the air and release it in the soil through nodules on its roots. It has a high protein content of 24 to 26 percent. In the eastern United States, farmers usually get three cuttings a year from each field. On some of the irrigated fields in sunny California, they can get up to seven cuttings a year. Alfalfa is a favored food of deer and elk.

All-terrain vehicles

ATVs are mechanized pack horses, allowing hunters to get back into country with their gear where they could not go on foot. It also allows big game species, like moose and elk, to be brought out when horses are not available. Many state and federal lands do not allow the use of ATVs, or mechanized vehicles of any kind. That's also to the good, because the ATV, if not properly used, causes a lot of erosion and disturbs wildlife.

Allen's Rule

Allen's Rule states that, among warm-blooded creatures, the physical extremities—ears, tails, legs—are shorter in the

The Coues white-tailed deer has larger ears for its size than the other whitetail subspecies.

coldest part of their range than in the warmest part. This rule is borne out by the Coues white-tailed deer of southern Arizona, which have much larger ears and tail (compared to body size) than do northern deer.

Alluvial plain

The depositing of sediment at the mouth of a river creates an alluvial plain, which results in the very rich soil found there. Deer will feed heavily in such areas because the vegetation is rich in nutrients.

Ambient temperature

The general, overall, outside temperature in the immediate area is known as the ambient temperature. To get an accurate ambient temperature reading, the thermometer should be in a well-ventilated, sheltered container five feet above the ground.

Amniotic fluid

The fluid inside the amniotic sac that surrounds and protects the developing fetus while it is being carried inside the female's uterus.

Annual recruitment

The number of young that survive for a period of one year. Under optimum conditions, a white-tailed deer herd can increase its population 40 percent per year. On the other hand, the recruitment rate for moose varies from 8 to 18 percent, according to range conditions, weather, and predation.

A white-tailed doe and her two six-month-old fawns. The fawns will be the annual recruitment.

Anthrax

Anthrax is a deadly infectious disease caused by a bacteria, *Bacillus anthrais.* It is a disease that is usually found in cattle and occasionally in deer and can cause death in humans. It is usually controlled in cattle by vaccination. It can be picked up from the soil or transmitted by biting flies. Overpopulations of deer are most susceptible, but as it is closely monitored, it is seldom a problem in this county. Saddam Hussein of Iraq has produced tons of anthrax material to be used in biological warfare.

Anthropomorphic

This is a term used to describe wildlife that has been given human form or characteristics. Many of our children's books and stories tell of such animals. The story of Bambi, the young deer that experienced the world as a human would, is one of the best-known examples.

Anti-hunter

As more people move away from the farm to live in the city, they lose contact with the soil and their roots. Whereas hunting, for many people, used to be a necessity, today, for most people, it is an option. Most people living in suburban areas today are neither hunters nor anti-hunters. Many understand that game animals are a renewable resource whose populations must be controlled. These folks understand that regulated sport hunting is the wildlife managers' most effective population control measure. The anti-hunters do not understand that basic concept. Dr. John Applegate, working with polling experts from Rutgers University's Eagleton Institute of Politics, found, "The greatest opposition to hunting comes from college age females living in urban areas who know nothing about wildlife."

Antler farming

A lucrative market has developed in many parts of the world for elk antlers that are removed from the animal while they are still in velvet. Some Far Eastern markets will pay up to $1,500 for a really large set of elk antlers in velvet, which are used for making medicine. Today there are many huge elk farms in New Zealand as well as in the United States.

A disadvantage to such farms, if their holding areas are not large enough, is that the elk become crowded and live on contaminated ground. Such conditions make the animals susceptible to disease; in fact, chronic wasting disease has been traced to several elk farms in the United States. To protect our wild herds of elk and deer, the federal and state governments are putting stringent laws and inspections in place.

Antler regression

White-tailed bucks mature at four years of age, and if they have access to sufficient nutritious food, their antlers will get larger until they are eight or nine years old. Then, as their teeth begin to wear out, the bucks can no longer process the

As bucks pass their prime, their antlers become smaller with fewer points, like this old mule deer buck.

food they eat as efficiently as they did when they were younger and their antler size will diminish or regress.

Antlered does

A doe having antlers is the result of her having more of the male sex hormone, testosterone, in her system than is normal. Part of this may be caused by genetics, because the percentages are higher in some areas than in others. It usually affects about 1 out of every 2,000 to 4,000 does. It also varies in the degree of "maleness" that is present. Usually a doe that has antlers that stay in velvet and do not harden is capable of bearing fawns. Usually, but not always, if a doe's antlers harden and the velvet is peeled off, she is not capable of becoming pregnant.

Antlers

Antlers are true bone growth, composed of calcium, phosphorus, and magnesium, that are formed on pedicel bases on the frontal skull plate of deer, elk, moose, and caribou. They are nourished by a network of external blood vessels in a "furry" velvet on the outside of the antler. They are one of the fastest-growing forms of tissue, with a mature buck adding up to ¼ inch of antler per day. A mature bull moose may add up to ½ inch of antler per day. The antlers usually start their new growth around the first of April, are fully developed and start to solidify by the first of August, and are rubbed clean of velvet around the first of September. They are cast, or shed, every year.

Aquatic vegetation

Vegetation that grows in water, such as the various types of water lilies, is known as aquatic vegetation. Both deer and moose feed heavily upon aquatic vegetation of many types.

Arizona white-tailed deer

See *Coues white-tailed deer.*

Arthropods

Arthropods are jointed-limbed creatures, such as crustaceans like lobsters, crabs, arachnids, and insects such as ticks. Ticks are parasites that are often just a nuisance to deer, but in some cases, heavy infestations can even cause death. It is the deer tick that transfers the spirochetes of Lyme disease from the deer to human beings. See *Lyme disease.*

Artificial insemination

This is the impregnation of does artificially rather than normally by a buck. This practice has long been used with cattle because farmers and ranchers can improve their herds by purchasing semen from a prize bull when they cannot afford to buy the bull. This practice is now being used with deer in an effort to produce larger-bodied, larger-antlered bucks. Outstanding white-tailed bucks have been sold as breeders for as much as one hundred thousand dollars and more. The semen from one ejaculation of such a prize buck may be divided into fifty vials that sell for as much as fifteen hundred dollars per vial. Artificial insemination of deer is big business today.

Artiodactyla

The deer is in the order Artiodactyla, meaning even-toed, because it has four toes on each foot. The deer has two main hooves, corresponding to our middle and ring fingers, and two dewclaws, corresponding to our index and pinky fingers. The deer's toes are known as metacarpals.

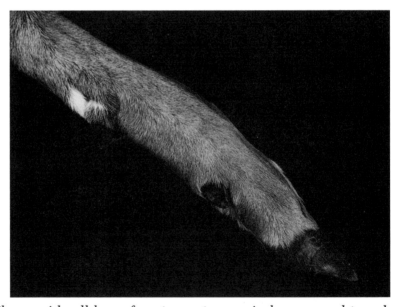

The cervids all have four toes—two main hooves and two dewclaws.

Atrophy

The old saying of "use it or lose it" is true. Any part of the body that is not used constantly atrophies. The appendix in humans and the metatarsal gland in deer are glands that are atrophying because of lack of use. See *Metatarsal gland.*

Attractant scents

There are many commercial scents being sold to hunters that are attractive to deer and can be used to lure the deer within bow or gun range. The scents are used to stimulate the deer's different appetites. White oak acorn scent involves the deer's hunger. Estrus scents spur the deer sexually. Anise scent invites a deer's curiosity.

Autoloading rifles

Autoloading rifles, although fast in action, have never been as popular as autoloading shotguns. The firing of the cartridge causes a piston to eject the spent casing and pump a fresh cartridge into the chamber in just a split second. The drawback is that the piston action does not allow this type of rifle to be chambered for as powerful cartridges as the bolt-action.

Autoloading shotguns

Although autoloading rifles have never been widely used, autoloading shotguns are very popular as they have a very fast action. The firing of the chambered shell harnesses the recoil of the fixed shell to drive the action backward so that the spent hull is ejected as a fresh shell is levered into the chamber. The internal hammer is cocked by the same action. The gun can be fired as fast as you can pull the trigger. According to the game being hunted, state and federal laws usually limit the number of shells that can be fired to three. A wooden plug inserted into the tubular magazine does the job.

Automobile fatalities

Collisions between automobiles and deer, elk, and moose take a tremendous toll each year. In some states, such as

Pennsylvania, as many as 48,000 deer are killed on the highways in a single year. According to the Insurance Information Institute, there are now more than 500,000 deer/car collisions nationwide each year, resulting in more than one billion dollars in damage each year. More than 200,000 people are injured annually, with over 200 killed. In the state of Maine, there were 2,126 moose/car accidents in the years 1996–1998.

Avery Island white-tailed deer (*O. v. mcilhennyi*)

This subspecies of whitetail is found along the Gulf coast of Texas and Louisiana. It is a good-sized deer with a very dark brown winter coat.

Two magnificent Avery Island white-tailed bucks.

B

Bachelor groups

The males of the deer family usually segregate themselves from the females and their young during the spring and summer and form bachelor groups. They rejoin the females prior to the rutting season, and in winter may be forced into the same areas as the females due to yarding or food shortages.

A bachelor group of white-tailed bucks. Credit: Irene Vandermolen

Backpack

If you plan to spend all day in the woods, you might want to carry a light backpack. The larger pack will carry everything a fanny pack will carry, including your drag rope, extra clothing, fire lighting equipment, binoculars, and other essentials.

Baiting

Baiting is usually thought of as the placing of shelled corn, sugar beets, carrots, apples, or other food in an effort to lure deer within shooting range. Hunting from an oak tree or at the edge of an alfalfa field might also be considered baiting from a strictly ethical point of view.

More and more states are allowing the use of baits in hunting deer in an effort to increase the kill and control exploding deer populations. Is hunting over a placed bait any different from hunting over a planted farm crop?

Balance of nature

This is one of the most misused, misunderstood phrases you are likely to hear bandied around about wildlife. Very few things are ever in balance in nature. What actually occurs is more like a pendulum swinging, a pendulum that never stops. The term is usually used to describe a predator-prey or an herbivore-habitat relationship. When predators are numerous they will reduce, but almost never eliminate, their prey species. When prey species become scarce, the predators starve or have fewer young. When the predator population is low, the prey species can increase. The same thing happens with the herbivores and their habitat. Instead of a balance, life is a series of checks and counterbalances.

Ballistics

Charts are available that give the performance of different caliber rifles, their bullet shapes, bullet weight, foot-pounds of energy when the bullet leaves the gun, foot-pounds delivered to the target at different ranges, and the trajectory of the bullet at different distances. The knowledge of ballistics is extremely important to every shooter who hopes to get the greatest accuracy from his gun. What is not usually listed, but is also important, is the grains of the different kinds of powder propelling the actual bullet. This information is needed by anyone who hand-loads his own ammunition. It is not listed on the ballistics charts because factory ammunition uses a standardized load for each bullet weight.

Bambi syndrome

This syndrome comes from the misconception that all wildlife is cute and cuddly and shares human attributes. It gets its name from the Walt Disney anthropomorphic movie about a whitetail buck fawn.

Barren female

In areas where the deer population has outgrown its food supply, many hunters—upon seeing does not being followed by fawns—assume that the doe is barren (not capable of reproducing). Does are almost never barren, except during advanced old age. Does that are deprived of sufficient nutritious food either do not conceive at all or drop malnourished fawns that are stillborn or die shortly thereafter.

Barren ground caribou (*R. t. groenlandicus*)

This caribou subspecies, also known as the tundra caribou, is found in Canada's Northwest Territories.

A barren ground caribou bull.

Basal metabolic rate

The conversion of food ingested to energy needed to maintain the normal body functions required to maintain life is known as the basal metabolic rate. It is usually calculated when the animal is at rest. Increased activity speeds up the process. An adult deer requires about 2,000 calories of food per day in warm weather. Running for an extended period of time can increase that need to up to 6,000 calories. In the winter, the BMR of all members of the deer family slows down drastically as a survival factor.

Bean pole woods

When an area is being reforested and the brush grows beyond the reach of deer, the thin saplings are known as "bean poles."

Bed

The compressed areas of leaves or vegetation made by the bodies of members of the deer family are known as their

A deer bed in snow.

beds. Elk, caribou, and moose will lie down in fresh snow, whereas deer will paw a hollow before they bed down in the snow.

Bedding area

Members of the deer family spend 60 to 70 percent of their time bedded down. Because they are ruminants, they gather a lot of food quickly when they are more susceptible to danger. They then retire to a safe area, their bedding area, which is usually in good cover, where they can rest and chew their cuds. Deer often bed in their feeding areas at night and retire to their bedding areas at dawn.

Bell

The bell on a moose may be a flap of skin or a rope-like piece of skin hanging down beneath the moose's chin. Despite the

The pendulous flap of skin hanging from a moose's throat is known as a "bell." Credit: James Keith Rue

network of blood vessels in this skin, the long, rope-like bell often freezes off in extremely cold weather. Both sexes may have bells.

Benchrest

A benchrest can be as simple as a three-foot board with two upright pieces in which Vs are cut to hold your rifle while you sight it in. The idea of a benchrest is to avoid human error by moving as little as possible as you set your sights. There are commercial benchrests that include leather pads, vise grips, and other features. They do a fine job, but anything that will help steady your rifle will do just fine.

Bergmann's Rule

This rule states that the farther a geographic race is found north or south of the equator, the larger the mass of its body will be. The larger the body mass, the smaller its relative surface area, resulting in a reduced loss of body heat. The Key deer of tropical Florida is our smallest deer, while the northern woodland and Dakota deer are our largest.

Bering Sea land bridge

During the periods when glaciers covered most of the northern sections of North America, so much water was trapped in the inland ice that the oceans were much lower, and a bridge of land was exposed across the Bering Sea linking Siberia to Alaska. The elk, caribou, and moose emigrated from Eurasia to North America during that period. Our deer evolved on this continent.

Bez tine

On elk and red deer, the first tine on the antler beam is known as the brow tine; the second tine is called the bez tine. These two tines on both beams produce the four tines that are often called "dogcatchers."

Bezoar stone

A bezoar stone—also called a calculus or madstone—is formed by layers of calcium or resinous material building up around some indigestible object such as a hairball. They are usually found in the reticulum. They may be more common than generally thought because few, if any, hunters look through the stomach contents for them. They may be found in all ruminants.

Bifurcate

Bifurcate means to split into branched parts. The best example of this is the branched tines on a mule deer's antlers.

It is most unusual for a whitetail's antlers to split, or bifurcate.

Binocular vision

We humans, as well as animals like wolves, cougars, and bears, are grouped as predators, and we have eyes on the front of our heads, which allows overlapping vision from each eye. This type of vision allows the predator to more accurately estimate distance, which is extremely important in capturing prey.

Biodiversity

For the optimum quantity and quality of wildlife, an area should have a wide variety of habitats that will allow the greatest number of diverse creatures to flourish. The greater the diversity, the better the chances of all species to flourish. There should also be a large enough number within a single species to provide a gene pool large enough to prevent inbreeding.

Biomass

This term is usually meant to cover the entire range of forage, or food, available to the different species of the deer family.

Biopolitics

It is unfortunate that, in many states today, the management of wildlife has been taken from the control of those who have been trained to manage it and put into the hands of the politicians who make laws about wildlife that are based on political pressure from their constituents instead of on a sound biological basis.

Bipod

A bipod is a two-legged shooting support that fastens on the end of your rifle's forearm. Some bipods have adjustable legs so that they reach the ground in either the prone or sitting position. A bipod greatly steadies your gun, allowing you to shoot much more accurately.

Birthing territory

No member of the deer family actually has a territory; they have home ranges. The one exception is the white-tailed doe, which will select an area in which to give birth to her new fawns. She will drive all other deer, including her previous year's fawns, from this territory. She will defend the territory for a period of three to four weeks, after which it is abandoned as she and her new fawns rejoin her maternal group. A birthing territory causes the does and their fawns to be scattered over the widest area possible, cutting down on losses by predation. By keeping all other does away, the mother ensures that her fawns imprint only on her.

White-tailed does maintain a "birthing territory" for two to three weeks.

Black flies

Small black flies of the family Simuliidae. Common in the North Woods, where they hatch out in cold-water streams. Often found by the thousands, they can make life a hell in the months of June and July.

Blackbeard Island whitetail (*O. v. nigribarbis*)

This subspecies is found on the Georgia islands of Blackbeard and Sapelo.

Blaze-orange

A bright, phosphorescent shade of orange. Today, by law, most gun hunters must wear blaze-orange hats and jackets while hunting. The bright color, which is easily seen by man, but not by game animals, has greatly reduced the number of hunting accidents that occur.

Bleat

The high-pitched call given by the fawns of deer. It closely resembles the bleat of a lamb. The pitch and intensity of the call varies greatly according to the fawn's needs and constitutes a language between the fawn and the doe. Despite this, a doe cannot recognize her own fawn by voice alone. She confirms its identity by smell.

Blood

The average 175-pound deer has the same amount of blood as a man of that weight, about seven pints. It takes a loss of three pints for a deer to go down from blood loss.

Blood sign

The average white-tailed deer weighing 150 to 175 pounds has seven pints of blood. The deer must lose three pints before it will die from blood loss. Bright red blood found in tracking usually indicates blood from an artery or vein. A bright, frothy, pink color is indicative of blood from the lungs. Dark blood, sometimes with a greenish tinge, is from the liver or stomach area.

Blue tongue

Blue tongue is a common name given to the diseases caused by any of seven viruses that cause that condition, or the epizootic hemorrhagic diseases. The symptoms of the diseases are almost identical. The spreading vectors are biting midges, which are killed by the cold, halting the spread of the disease each year. Deer with the disease develop blue tongues and bleed internally right through the walls of the various organs. The blood that leaks through is thin and yellow in color. Most deer die within 72 hours of being infected. This disease cannot be transmitted to humans.

Body language

Most of the communication among members of the deer family is done through body language or postures. The "hard

The "hard stare" aggressive approach of white-tailed bucks is body language.

stare" is a sign of extreme aggression in the whitetail, black-tail, and mule deer. In this posture, the buck's head is out-stretched forward and held lower than his back, his chin is tucked in, his antlers are projected forward, his ears are laid straight back, his body hair stands on end, he walks with a stiff-legged gait, and his tongue may be flicked in and out of his mouth.

A bull moose walks with a stiff-legged gait with his body and head rocking from side to side, showing the size of his antlers. His bell will flap back and forth, his eyes will be rolled up so that the whites are showing, and his mane will be fully erected.

Body size

Each animal knows exactly how big both his antlers and body size are and how he stacks up against his rival. Usually the animal with the largest body will also have the largest antlers and is usually the dominant animal. Hunters can learn to tell a trophy animal by its body size, as a deep body denotes maturity.

Bolt-action rifle

The most popular rifle today is the bolt-action. Its locking lugs allow for more powerful cartridges to be used than either a lever or pump action. The bolt is usually on the right side of the gun, but it can be gotten on the left, for left-handers, in some makes and models. The strength and rigidity of the bolt-action allow for great accuracy, and the bolt can be worked fast with practice, but it does take a lot of practice. More calibers and bullets are available for bolt-action rifles than for any other type. This is the rifle used by most hunters today.

Bolt-action shotgun

Bolt-action shotguns have never really been popular in this country because they are so much slower to reload. They have a single barrel and a shell is lifted from the tubular magazine into the barrel and then seated in the chamber by working the bolt forward and back. That action also cocks the hammer, which may be exposed or internal.

Bolus

A bolus, or cud, is a mass of vegetation that members of the deer family regurgitate from the paunch, or rumen, back up into the mouth to be thoroughly re-chewed before being swallowed for the second time. An adult deer's bolus is about the size of a small lemon.

Bonding

When the females of the deer family give birth to their young, they wash them thoroughly with their tongues. This removes the odor of the amniotic fluid and imprints the young's odor on their mother. The odor of the mother's saliva helps the fawn imprint on, or bond with, its mother. Adult deer, in both matriarchal and fraternal groups, groom one another, establishing bonds of family or friendship.

Social grooming is a bonding action.

Bone marrow

The color and fat content of the bone marrow in deer is a good indicator of the health of the animal. When the marrow is pure white, the fat content is usually higher than 90 percent and the deer is in excellent health. As the animals are on restricted food in the winter in the north, the fat is utilized from the bones as energy and changes in color from white to yellow to pink to red. The red marrow has only five percent fat and is proof the animal starved to death.

Bone saw

A bone saw can be used to cut through the vertebrae of big game animals to quarter them. I do not believe that a bone saw should be used to cut hams into steaks, because I believe that all meat should be bone-free. It is the fat in the marrow in the center of the bone that goes rancid quickly, even when frozen. I do all my butchering with just a boning knife.

Boone & Crockett Club

The Boone & Crockett Club was named after Daniel Boone and David Crockett. It was founded in 1887 by Theodore Roosevelt and a group of his sportsman friends. The club is the official register and keeper of the records of all of the big game species in North America. They have constantly fought for the conservation of wildlife and the ethical hunting of wildlife.

Boreal forest

The forested areas found in the northern sections of North America and Eurasia. The taiga is the area where the trees thin out and become dwarfed and is the intermediate area between the boreal forest and the treeless tundra.

Brainworm

The meningeal worm, *Parelaphostrongylus tenuis,* is also called the brainworm. The white-tailed deer usually is infected with, but not affected by, this parasite. The parasites live in the deer's brain; their eggs hatch out in the deer's lungs and the larvae are passed out in the deer's feces. Snails and slugs pick up the larvae on the vegetation they eat. The larvae from the snails then get into the bloodstream of the moose and elk and migrate to the brain, where they can be fatal to both animals. It is only because the eastern moose are beginning to build up an immunity to the brainworm, like the white-tailed deer have, that the moose population is finally increasing.

Breeding season

The breeding season of all members of the deer family is governed by photoperiodism, the amount of light in a 24-hour period that is picked up by the pineal gland. The timing of the breeding season is critical and the "window of opportunity" in the north is short because the young must be born the following year at the optimum time for survival, which is governed by warm weather and growing vegetation. In the south, the breeding season is longer and later, and timing is not as critical.

Broomed

Shrubs and bushes that are repeatedly browsed, that have all of their new growth nipped off year after year, grow very bushy tops and are said to be "broomed."

Brow tine

On deer and elk, the first antler growing on the main beam on either side of the head is referred to as the brow tine, eye tine, or G-1 tine.

Browse

The new year's growth on the end of a woody twig or branch is referred to as browse. Deer and moose are primarily browsers, while elk and caribou are primarily grazers. However, all of these species, at times, will either browse or graze according to the food that is available.

This buck has exceptionally long brow tines.

Overbrowsing by deer destroys habitat, not only for deer but for many other types of wildlife also.

Browse line

When deer or elk become overpopulated, they browse on all of the tender woody twigs as high as they can reach. Often standing on their hind legs to reach the overhead branches, deer destroy all vegetation as high as seven feet above the ground, while elk create a line at about ten feet. When these animals create a browse line, it is often referred to as highlining. A browse line is proof positive of the overpopulation of the species.

Brucellosis

A disease, caused by the bacterium *Brucella abortus,* that causes cattle to abort their young. Deer have been blamed for spreading the disease to cattle. Research shows this claim to be absolutely false.

Buck

The male gender of the whitetail, blacktail, and mule deer are always referred to as bucks.

Buck fever

Buck fever is an affliction of the human nervous system caused by anxiety, apprehension, excitement, lack of confidence, and so on. It manifests itself in many ways. The hunter may not be able to raise a gun or bow to shoot because he or she is shaking so badly, or may not be able to move at all. Some hunters have been known to pump all of their shells through their guns without ever firing them. Archery hunters have been known to nock and then drop their arrows without drawing the arrow back.

Buck fever is usually an affliction of novice hunters upon seeing their first deer approach. With time and expertise, most hunters get over buck fever; a few unfortunate ones do not.

Buck rubs

The rubs or scarring done on saplings or brush by all of the members of the deer family are known as rubs; those done by bucks are buck rubs. The rubs are first made to remove the velvet from the antlers. Thereafter, the rubs are made as scent stations, while the whitened areas are a form of visual communication. The rubs are also done to strengthen the animal's neck muscles in preparation for the fights to come.

Buckshot

Buckshot comes in seven sizes, measuring 24/100 of an inch for No. 4 to 36/100 of an inch for No. 000. Naturally, you get more pellets in the same size shell when using No. 4 than when using No. 000. A longer shot shell or a larger gauge will give more pellets than will a short shell. For example, in 12-gauge, a 2¾-inch shell has 12 pellets of No. 00 buckshot, a 3-inch shell has 15 pellets, and a 3½-inch shell has 18 pellets. Buckshot should not be used at distances of more than 30 yards.

Buffer zone

Diversionary crops are sometimes planted to keep deer from feeding in areas where they are not wanted. I do not consider buffer zones to be practical, as I have found they often tend to concentrate unwanted animals.

Bugle

The bellowed, high-pitched, challenging call of the bull elk is known as bugling.

Bull elk bugling during the rutting season. Credit: Len Rue, Jr.

Bull

Male caribou, elk, and moose are referred to as bulls. Rarely, someone may refer to a male caribou as a buck.

Bullet shape

A round-nosed bullet usually has better expansion than a larger, tapering bullet. A tapered bullet is more accurate for long-distance shooting.

Bull's Island white-tailed deer (*O. v. taurinsulae*)

This very limited subspecies of the whitetail is found only on Bull's Island, South Carolina.

Burr

The widened base of an antler just above where the antler grows from the pedicel is known as the burr or coronet.

Burro mule deer (*O. h. eremicus*)

This subspecies, found in the extreme southeastern portion of California and from southwestern Arizona down into Mexico, is smaller than the Rocky Mountain mule deer and much lighter in coloration.

Butchering

The term used for the cutting up of the meat of game animals that have been shot. Cleanliness and the proper butchering of the carcass can make all the difference in producing delicious meat that does not have a "gamey" taste. Those of us who have been raised in the country usually butcher our own meat, while many hunters today take their game to professional butchers.

Butterfat

The amount of actual fat found in milk. It is usually found in the cream. Holstein cows usually give 3.5 percent butterfat;

Jersey and Guernsey cows give about 6 percent. All members of the deer family produce about 10.5 percent butterfat. On this rich milk, the young gain weight and strength rapidly.

Button buck

At about four months of age, little buck fawns begin to grow calcified bumps on their forehead skull plates that will form the pedicels that will be the bases for their future antlers. At six months of age, the pedicels are about ½ an inch high and, although still skin-covered, very noticeable. These little fellows are referred to as button bucks. Only rarely, under the most optimum conditions, do the seven- to eight-month-old bucks produce little ½-inch antlers.

The pedicels are forming on this seven-month-old buck's skull plate, making him a "button buck."

C

Cactus bucks

Bucks that have been castrated, either deliberately or accidentally, after their antlers have started to grow are not able to produce hardened antlers. The soft antlers usually freeze off. If there is any further antler growth, it will often be shaped like a conical beehive and the deer will be referred to as a cactus buck.

Calcification

Antlers usually start to grow around the first of April. They are covered in velvet and grow throughout April, May, June, and July. Most antlers have reached their maximum size around the first of August, when the burr grows outward, beginning to shut off the blood supply to the velvet. The antlers begin to solidify, to calcify or harden, from the base to the tips. They have usually completed their calcification by the first week in September, and the velvet is rubbed off shortly thereafter.

Caliber

The caliber of a rifle or a pistol is measured in the precise diameter of the bullet. The designations are done in hundredths or thousandths of an inch or in millimeters. For example, the .22-caliber bullet measures exactly twenty-two one hundredths of an inch. A .45-caliber measures forty-five one hundredths of an inch. A .243 measures two hundred forty-three one thousandthsof an inch. The famed .30/06 is a .30-caliber bullet whose load was perfected in 1906. The old .45/70 is forty-five one hundredths of an inch in diameter pushed by 70 grains of powder.

California mule deer (*O. h. californicus*)

This deer is found only in California from the Sierras to the Pacific. It integrates with the Columbian black-tailed deer along the northern border of its range. It is smaller than the Rocky Mountain mule deer and also has a smaller white rump patch.

A California mule deer buck in velvet.

Calling deer

Calling deer has been practiced by the Indians for thousands of years. The first commercial deer call came on the market about forty years ago and was patterned on a call that the West Coast Indians used to call black-tailed deer. Today, hunters use grunt tubes, real and plastic antlers, rattling bags, and electronic game calls. All of these calls are designed to imitate the sounds that deer make and most of them are very effective—some of the time.

Calling elk

Everyone is familiar with the high-pitched bugling call of the bull elk. Most calls have been designed to imitate that particular call. Today, more and more hunters are making the short barking call made by the cow elk. This often gets a better response from a bull than does a bull call because the cow is what the bull is actually interested in.

Calling moose

Moose inhabit such densely forested northern regions that it is nearly impossible to see them in the first place. Hunters go to areas that moose are known to frequent and then get on the downwind side of an open lake area. Imitating the sound of a cow moose, the hunters attempt to lure the bull out into the open so he can be seen. The Indians made megaphones, cones of birch bark, that they used to get the sound of their calling out farther. An old Algonquin told me to fill the megaphone with water, hold it high and let the water trickle out into the lake to imitate a cow urinating.

A cow moose and calf. Credit: Len Rue, Jr.

Calves

The young of elk, caribou, and moose are referred to as calves.

Camera

You cannot hunt and do wildlife photography at the same time. If you want to photograph a game species, do so while you are scouting before the season opens. If you want to record your kill on film, there are many good little "point-and-shoot" cameras that can be tucked in your pack. The photos in this book are taken with long professional lenses that no hunter will carry in the field. Wildlife photography is how I make my living.

Camouflage clothing

The first camouflage clothing was produced for the Armed Forces during World War II. The camouflage clothing offered to hunters today is far superior, as the many patterns are more realistically designed to match specific backgrounds at different times of the year. As I try to photograph wildlife 365 days of the year, I dress in camouflage 365 days of the year.

Camouflage clothing should not be worn if you go to other countries. In most countries, only the military wear camouflage. Camouflage clothing is illegal to wear during the gun season in most states, when blaze-orange must be worn for safety's sake. Some states allow the use of blaze-orange camouflage.

Canine teeth

Canine teeth are the four long, sharp, recurring teeth in the front of the mouths of all members of the canine and feline families of animals. They are used for grasping prey. The canine teeth of the members of the deer family are not the meat-piercing teeth of the predators. The deer's canines so closely resemble the incisor teeth that they are often classified and counted as such.

Most bowhunters wear camouflage clothing, while gun hunters must use blaze-orange.

Occasionally deer have what are known as maxillary canine teeth in the upper jaw. These are very rare. Southern deer are more apt to have these canine teeth than northern deer. Bull elk frequently have these canine teeth, known as the "ivory," and they are eagerly sought by hunters.

Canopy

When the trees in a forest grow large enough that their branches form a green roof, preventing the sunlight from reaching the forest floor, that covering is known as a canopy.

Caping

Great care must be taken when the skin of a trophy animal is removed if the head is to be mounted. It is best to cut the skin behind the shoulders and skin up to the head, and then have a skilled taxidermist skin out the head. The ears and lips must be skinned and turned, and it requires experience to do a good job. Remove the skin and head and freeze them if you can't get them to a taxidermist within a day or so.

Carbohydrates

Sugars and starches are good examples of the energy-rich, fat-producing compounds known as carbohydrates.

Carmen Mountain white-tailed deer (*O. v. carminis*)

This small deer is found in the Big Bend region of Texas and Mexico. It is isolated from other subspecies by the surrounding deserts.

A Carmen Mountain white-tailed spike buck in velvet.

Carrying capacity

This has long been a term used to describe how many deer a given area can support without the range being destroyed by overpopulation. It is usually calculated that one square mile of good habitat will support twenty deer under optimum conditions.

Casting

When the antlers of members of the deer family fall off, they are said to be cast.

Castration

The removal of the male's testicles either by surgery or by an accident. This renders the male sterile, not inclined or able to breed.

Cellulose

The main carbohydrates making up the walls of the cells in green plants. A major source of energy for members of the deer family. The larger elk and moose can convert cellulose to energy more efficiently than can the smaller deer.

Cementum

A harder-than-bone layer built up in annual layers in the teeth of animals. A cross sectioning of the teeth allows these layers to be counted accurately, aging the animal. See *Aging by the teeth.*

Cervidae

In the scientific classification of mammals, all members of the deer group are listed in the family Cervidae.

Cervus

Cervus was the Latin name given in 1758 by Carolus Linnaeus, the father of taxonomy, to the Swedish red deer, which he called *Cervus elaphus.* Cervus comes from the family name Cervidae. *Cervus elaphus* is the Latin name that is given to all of the North American elk because they are directly related to the European red deer.

Chemical signposts

The most effective way for deer to communicate is through the use of chemical signposts. The deer do not have to actually see each other for their messages to be relayed, and they are effective for hours, days, or even weeks, until the scent is dissipated by the weather. The deer put their glandular scent on overhead branches, rubs, scrapes, and other areas. The messages convey who left them, their sex, their dominance ranking, what they have been eating, and so on.

A white-tailed buck rubbing an overhead stick against his forehead scent gland.

Choke tube

See *Polychoke.*

Circadian rhythm

Regular patterns of activity that occur during a 24-hour cycle. In deer, this would refer to their feeding and bedding activities during the times they are not hunted.

Circumpolar

Meaning "around the world," circumpolar refers to the fact that moose are found in the boreal forests and caribou and reindeer are found in the tundra regions all around the world.

Clear-cuts

Clear-cuts are forested areas where no tree is left standing after being timbered.

Clear-cutting of forests is usually done in blocks.

Climax forest

The third or last step in forest regeneration. After a forest has been clear-cut, new seedlings or brush starts to grow. Within 15 to 20 years, the brush has grown to the "bean pole" or sapling stage. When the trees mature, they form a climax forest.

Climbing spurs

Climbing spurs are like the devices worn by telephone repair-men to climb telephone poles. However, do not use lineman's climbing spurs to climb trees because the shank of the spurs is only 1 to 1½ inches in length, which is okay for them because all of the bark has been removed from the poles. You must use tree-climbing spurs that have 3-inch spurs, which are long enough to penetrate the bark and grip into the wood beneath it.

Cloven hoof

The toes of the members of the deer family correspond to our four fingers and are called cloven hooves. The horse has a single, or unsplit, hoof.

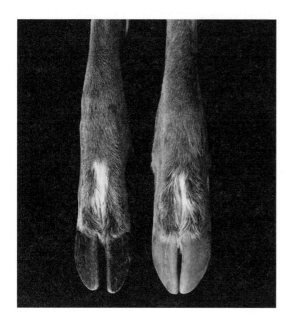

The cloven hooves of white-tailed deer. The one on the left has normal coloration, while the one on the right lacks pigment.

Cohabitating

Deer are said to be cohabitants of a forest when deer, fox, bobcats, birds, and other animals also live there.

Colonization

When I was a young man guiding canoe trips into the wilds of Quebec, Canada, I saw the white-tailed deer expand their range northward about one hundred miles in ten years' time as the virgin forests were cut and the wolf and moose populations displaced. The deer were colonizing areas in which they had never been found before.

Colostrum

The thick, yellow milk that a female mammal produces for the first three days after giving birth to her young is called colostrum milk. It is very important that all human and animal babies get this "mother's milk" because it contains antibodies to all of the diseases and infections to which the mother has been exposed. The colostrum effectively inoculates the baby against all of those diseases and infections.

Columbian black-tailed deer (*O. h. columbianus*)

This deer is found in California, Oregon, Washington, and British Columbia. It manages to thrive in dry chaparral and in the wettest, densest forests in North America. They are smaller than the other subspecies of mule deer and are distinguished by the top of their tail, which is covered with black hairs.

An especially fine Columbian black-tailed buck. Credit: Len Rue, Jr.

Columbian white-tailed deer
(*O. v. columbianus*)

This subspecies of the whitetail is listed as an endangered species. Its range has been so reduced that it is now found only in the federal wildlife refuge on the Columbia River near Cathlamet, Washington.

Combination gun

Many of the European drillings are a combination of two shotgun barrels and a rifle barrel. Many of the American combination guns have a rifle barrel on top and a shotgun barrel on the bottom. There is usually only a single trigger and a barrel selector switch. The combination guns are usually billed as "survival" guns and feature perhaps a .22 Hornet rifle and a 20-gauge shotgun.

Commensalism

When two different species live in the same area and one benefits from the other without causing it harm. For example, the whitetail greatly benefits from living in an area with a high porcupine population because the deer eat the hemlock tips and branches that the porcupines drop as they feed.

Commercial deer scents

There are many different kinds of commercial deer scents available today. All of the urine-based scents are from captive deer held on concrete floors so that the urine can be collected. Some scents are composed of food items that deer eat, such as apples and acorns. Some of the scents have various chemical ingredients that either are attractive to deer or arouse their curiosity.

Communication

In all communication, there must be both a sender and a receiver. With the members of the deer family, the communi-

A Texas white-tailed buck depositing saliva on an overhead branch at a scrape by chewing on the branch.

cation may be vocal or include other audible sounds. It may be visual, such as body language, gestures, or the whitened tree surfaces, or rubs. It may be olfactory, as in the uses of various gland secretions placed on their own bodies or in chemical signposts. Or it may be tactile, such as in social grooming, courtship, or foot stamping.

Compass

Most people do not know how to properly use the compass they carry, if indeed they carry one. The only thing you can count on is that the compass will point to magnetic north. A compass, if followed, will allow you to walk in a straight line. A compass, if followed carefully, will allow you to walk to a certain point and return if you exactly reverse the directions. It's seldom possible to walk a straight line because of the terrain. To properly use a compass and a map takes some training, as you have to be able to calculate declination to know the difference between the true north of the map and the magnetic north that your compass needle points to.

Compound bow

A compound bow is a modern hunting bow using pulleys, cams, or wheels that reduce the draw weight at full draw by 50 to 65 percent. This allows the hunter to pull a much more powerful bow and hold it while he sights than if he was using a straight bow. Today, 80 percent of bowhunters are using compound bows. They are made of many different materials, such as wood, fiberglass, or carbon, or a combination of those materials.

Concentrate feeders

Cattle are considered concentrate feeders because they eat a swath of different types of grasses or vegetation at one time.

Bison, like cattle, are concentrate feeders.

Conduction

When deer lose body heat by lying on cold ground.

Cone cells

A deer's eye and that of a human are basically the same. Light passes through the cornea and registers on the retina. The retina is composed of rod and cone cells. We humans have more cones than rods, which gives us sharper vision and the ability to see a wider range of color. Deer have more rods than cones and can see better in darkness than we can.

Coniferous

Referring to cone-bearing evergreen trees. They do not lose their needles, which are really leaves, in the fall.

Conspecific

Animals of the same species that inhabit the same range are conspecific.

Contraception

A means of preventing pregnancy. Because of the burgeoning white-tailed deer population, biologists are testing many types of contraceptives to be used on deer in areas where the population cannot be controlled by hunting.

They have tried oral contraceptives placed in food. They have tried injections delivered to the muscles by using hypodermic syringes powered by blowguns or dart guns. To date, these methods have not proved to be economically feasible.

Contralateral

Contra means opposite. In deer, if a foot or lower leg is injured on one side of the body, the buck's antlers are usually deformed on the opposite side.

Controlled burn

A fire that is deliberately set for land or habitat management reasons. Grass fires have always been a natural controller of forest encroachment on the grasslands. With fire suppression by man, much grassland is being taken over by forest. This is very important in elk country because the elk feed more upon grass than they browse.

Convection

Warm air rises because it is lighter in weight than cold air. When members of the deer family lose body heat in cold weather it is because of convection.

A bull elk copulating with the cow. Credit: Len Rue, Jr.

Copulation

The mating of creatures whereby the male impregnates the female by depositing his semen, via his penis, into her vagina so that her eggs can be fertilized.

Cornea

The outer, transparent layer of the eye. It corresponds to the front element of a lens.

Cornified

A process of changing living epithelial cells into a keratinized non-living structure such as your fingernails. A deer's hooves or the outer layers of animal horns are good examples of cornified cells.

Coronet

The outward growth at the base of a deer's antlers just above the portion joining the antler to the pedicel is known as the coronet or burr.

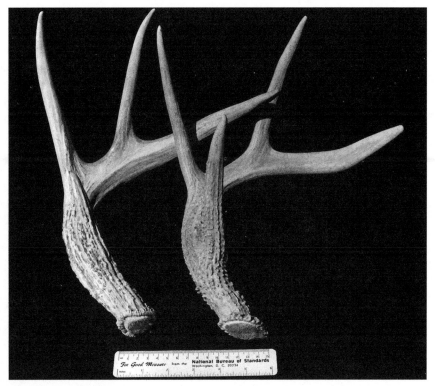

The coronet gets larger every year.

Corticoids

The odor of a dominant buck will cause a young buck's adrenal cortex to produce corticoids. The corticoids inhibit testicular growth and function, thus reducing the production of testosterone which, in turn, reduces the social stress of competition by the younger buck.

Coues white-tailed deer (*O. v. couesi*)

The Coues (pronounced "cows"), or Arizona whitetail, is a small subspecies. It has larger ears and tail in relation to its body size than most of the other whitetails. This deer is isolated in the mountains of southeastern California, southern Arizona, and southwestern New Mexico.

Cougar

The cougar, or mountain lion, is found primarily in the western states, although the Florida panther is also a cougar.

The cougar is slowly, but surely, increasing its range and population in the eastern part of the United States. In the western states, particularly where hunting has been banned, cougars have increased dramatically, as have their attacks on humans. The cougar is a major predator on the mule deer.

A cougar with a whitetail that it has killed.

Courtship

The adult males of all members of the deer family court the females to stimulate them and to increase their desire to breed. The males deposit scent on themselves, on the ground, or on trees to attract and stimulate the females. The males will rub their bodies against the females and often lick their vaginal areas. The false mounting and all of the courtship proceedings also help the female to ovulate so that her eggs will be in her uterus when breeding actually takes place.

This white-tailed buck is following a pre-estrus doe and will stay with her until she comes into heat.

Cover scents

There are a great many products available to aid in masking human odor. Deer urine is both an attractant and a cover scent. Fox urine helps to mask human scent, as does skunk's mercapton. Fresh earth is a good cover scent. Clothing is now available that uses charcoal to filter and nullify human scent. Chlorophyll tablets are eaten to reduce odors from the stomach. All of these products help, but as long as you breathe, you will give off human odor, and when you stop breathing, you will smell even worse.

Cow

Female elk, caribou, and moose are referred to as cows.

Coyote

The coyote is the most intelligent, most adaptable member of the canine family found in North America. The adult male of the western subspecies weighs about 35 to 40 pounds. The adult male of the eastern subspecies, because it also has wolf genes, weighs 45 to 50 pounds. The coyote is a noted predator of the white-tailed and mule deer, and particularly of the fawns.

Coyotes are large enough to kill even adult deer.

Crepuscular

A creature that becomes active when the daylight is beginning to fade to darkness is said to be crepuscular. Deer are crepuscular because most of them are very active at dusk and dawn.

Crop damage

A major problem with the large population of white-tailed deer in the United States is the millions of dollars of damage they do to farm crops. At a time when the family farmer is often struggling to survive, these losses can be catastrophic. It is to give such farmers much needed relief that many states have greatly liberalized their deer hunting seasons.

Corn is a favored food of deer, which frequently cause extreme crop damage.

Crossbow

The crossbow is a powerful weapon that has been used for more than a thousand years. It shoots a short arrow known as a bolt. It takes great pressure to cock a crossbow, but the string is then held back mechanically until it is released by pulling the trigger. They are legal for hunting in just a few states.

Crossbreeding

Young white-tailed deer usually disperse from their natal home range at the age of 1 to 1½ years. Research shows that most of them move beyond five miles. This prevents them from breeding with their female relatives. When they do breed, it will be with unrelated deer; this is known as crossbreeding.

This is a cross between a black-tailed doe and a white-tailed buck.

Crusting

When the top layer of snow melts and then freezes, it often forms a crust that will support the weight of predators, but not the deer. Crusted snow puts deer at a tremendous disadvantage, as they often break through the crust.

Cryptic coloration

The young of both deer and elk have spotted coats that aid in their concealment. The white spots on a red background look like the sun's pattern on the forest floor. Any coloration that has a camouflaging effect is known as cryptic coloration.

The spotted coat of this white-tailed fawn is known as cryptic coloration. Credit: Irene Vandermolen

Cud

See *Bolus.*

Culling

Culling is the removing of unwanted specimens in a herd in order to improve the herd or the habitat. When states liberalize the taking of female animals, it is a culling effort. Ordinarily, culling is most properly done on fenced-in, controlled lands.

Cursorial

All members of the deer family are considered to be cursorial animals because they have the long legs needed for running.

D

Dagger tine

The fourth tine on an elk's antler is usually the longest. This tine is often flattened and does the most damage to an opponent in a fight. It is referred to as the dagger tine.

The fourth tine on an elk's antlers is usually the longest. Credit: Len Rue, Jr.

Dakota white-tailed deer (*O. v. dacotensis*)

A very large deer ranging from North and South Dakota, parts of Nebraska, Kansas, Wyoming, and Montana to the Canadian provinces of Manitoba, Saskatchewan, and Alberta. The current world record buck, taken by Milo Hanson, is a Dakota whitetail. This subspecies has produced more record-class trophy deer than any other subspecies.

The Dakota whitetail is one of the largest sub-species.

Debarking

Although all members of the deer family remove the bark from saplings and bushes by rubbing them with their antlers, that is usually not known as debarking. Both elk and moose debark saplings by feeding heavily on the bark of the aspen, cutting and pulling strips of bark loose with their teeth.

Deciduous teeth

The first set of teeth that most mammals have are replaced with larger, stronger permanent teeth within a few years. These deciduous teeth are popularly known as "baby teeth," "milk teeth," or "puppy teeth."

Decoys

It has become popular for bow hunters to use deer decoys while hunting, as it gives the deer that is coming in something on which to focus its attention. Decoys that have movable tails are the most successful because deer are quick to see the slightest motion. I don't think it makes any difference whether you use a buck or a doe decoy.

Deer accidents

Deer, like humans, are subject to all types of accidents. In dashing through the woods, they may impale themselves on a jagged stick. They may get their antlers caught in trees they are rubbing. They may lose an eye in fighting. They may tangle their feet or antlers in fences they are trying to cross. In urban areas, they may get tangled in clotheslines or bad-

Deer frequently get their feet caught in fences they try to jump.

minton nets, drown in swimming pools, jump through picture windows, and so on. That's in addition to being struck by motor vehicles.

Deer drive

One of the most popular forms of deer hunting performed by clubs or groups. It consists of following a plan whereby an area is assigned, then a number of drivers walk through the area and attempt to push the deer past standers who are stationed along the perimeter of the area. The standers are all positioned before the drivers start. Don't get the idea that the deer can be driven; they can't. What the drivers actually do is push the deer out of their hiding places; the deer go where they want.

Deer repellents

In an effort to keep deer from eating their shrubbery, people have used a wide variety of repellents such as bags of human hair, blood meal, wolf urine, and bars of Ivory soap. There are also a number of commercial repellents on the market. Most repellents work for just a short time because the deer get used to the odors or the odors are diluted by the sun, rain, or snow.

Deer yards

Healthy adult deer can stand extreme cold; they cannot tolerate wind. High winds cause the deer to lose body heat rapidly. Northern deer gather in low-lying areas in dense swamps that usually have good conifer cover, thus breaking the force of the wind. Many of these deer yards are traditional, having been used by deer for hundreds of years. Deer often migrate 25 miles or more to yard up.

Deer pellets on a trail in an overbrowsed deer yard.

Defecation

In the spring, summer, and fall, when food is plentiful, deer usually defecate 30 to 36 times in a 24-hour period. During the winter, when food is scarce and the deer's metabolism has slowed, the deer will defecate 8 to 12 times a day.

Deme

A local population of blood-related animals.

Demographics

The study of a population, recording the births, deaths, and current status of all individuals.

Denude

When herbivores eat all of the available vegetation, they have denuded the area.

Desert mule deer (*O. h. crooki*)

This deer has the second largest range of any of the mule deer. It is adapted to live under the very harsh conditions found in the deserts of southern Arizona and New Mexico, west Texas, and hundreds of miles south in Mexico. It is a large-bodied deer, but it would be a good deal heavier if more nutritious food was available.

Desert mule deer bucks in velvet.

Dewclaws

All members of the deer family have just four toes; they lack the thumb. The toes corresponding to our middle and ring fingers are their two main hooves. The toes corresponding to our index and pinky fingers have shrunken and are located behind the main hooves; they are known as dewclaws. In deer and elk, the dewclaws seldom touch the ground or are seen in their tracks. The moose has larger dewclaws because it walks on swampy ground, and they help keep it from sinking in the mud. The caribou has the longest dewclaws of all because they walk on snow so much of the time. The caribou's dewclaws almost double the bearing surface of their hooves.

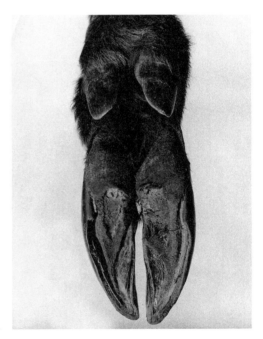

Right forefoot of a moose.

Diastema

All members of the deer family have a toothless gap between the eight front teeth of their lower jaw and their six premolars and six molars. That space is known as the diastema.

Diehl day

The number of daylight hours in a 24-hour period.

Digestible crude protein

Animal nutritionists use this phrase to describe what percentage of any particular food that a deer eats is available to its body. Deer need a diet of at least 16 percent protein to maximize body and antler growth. Alfalfa has a crude protein of 24 to 26 percent.

Digitigrade

Animals that walk on their toes, as do all of the canines and felines, are known as digitigrade animals.

Notice the difference in body size between this white-tailed buck and the doe.

Dimorphic

Because the males of all members of the deer family are so much larger than are the females, they are said to be dimorphic.

Dispersal

To prevent inbreeding (mating with family members), yearling bucks leave the area in which they were born and move a distance of about five miles. The young bucks are usually driven from the area by their mothers and other related adult females.

Diurnal

Wildlife that are most active during the daylight hours are said to be diurnal.

Diversity

A healthy environment will be home to a great many different species of birds, animals, and plants. The greater the diversity of species, the better the chance of survival for all.

DNA

Deoxyribonucleic acid is the carrier of the genetic information found in chromosomes. The code can be taken from any sample of a creature's body, such as hair, blood, saliva, or tissue. It is widely used in forensics for both humans and wildlife. Wildlife biologists can often identify the exact region from which a poached animal was taken.

Doe

The females of white-tailed, black-tailed, and mule deer are known as does.

Doe day

For years, when deer herds were being rebuilt after almost complete extirpation, it was only legal to hunt bucks. The idea behind the "bucks only" rule was the fact that most bucks are superfluous; one buck can breed six to eight does. When deer herds reached the carrying capacity of the land, many states opened up one special day when a doe could be

A Rocky Mountain mule deer doe.

taken. Today, in an effort to reduce the deer population, unlimited numbers of does can be taken, but only a single buck.

Dominance

Dominance is the driving force in a deer's life and that of almost every other creature. The dominant buck has the best chance of passing on his genes through breeding. It has access to the best areas, the best food, the best chance of survival. Dominance is never a static condition, but one that is in a constant flux; it can change day by day.

Double-barreled rifle

These rifles use the same break-open action as a double-barreled shotgun. They are usually made only in the largest of cartridges and are used on the most dangerous big game of Africa and Asia. Their main advantage is that two shots can be fired faster than with any other action.

The dominant buck on the left has the subordinate buck backing away.

Double-barreled shotgun

This is a gun commonly used by farm families because it can be used for both small game and deer. It has two barrels, side by side or one on top of the other, in the case of an "over-and-under." It is opened at the breech and the shells inserted or ejected. The hammers on all of the modern guns are internal. Most side-by-sides have two triggers; most over-and-unders have a single trigger.

Downwind

All members of the deer family rely most heavily on their keen sense of smell to detect danger. To avoid being discovered, you must constantly be alert to the direction of the wind and try to have the wind blow from the game to you. Being downwind of your game is the only sure way that they will not be able to smell you.

Drag rope

Most deer are gotten out of the woods by dragging the carcass using either a rope or a light aircraft cable. There are commercial drags sold that have built-in handles, and some even have a shoulder harness that works very well. Naturally it is easier to drag a deer carcass if the ground is covered with snow. Be careful not to drag out patches of hair if your buck is a trophy and you plan to have a shoulder mount done by a taxidermist.

Draw systems

Because there are not unlimited numbers of many types of game animals, restrictions are needed on the numbers of hunters allowed to hunt each particular species. All states allow their own hunters to hunt at very basic license fees. Out-of-state hunters pay much higher fees. For exceptionally scarce animals, such as wild sheep and grizzly bears, even residents must enter a lottery. Out-of-state hunters usually have to enter a lottery for most big game species, with whitetails often being the exception to this rule.

Drilling rifle

These rifles are used more in Europe than here in North America. They use the break-open action like the double rifle, with the difference being that they have a third barrel nestled right below the two side-by-side barrels. Usually a drilling gun will have its two main barrels as shotguns and the bottom barrel as a rifle.

Drivers

It takes real coordination for a line of drivers to keep a fairly straight line. For safety's sake, each driver should know where the rest of the drivers and standers are. Some groups like silent drives, where the drivers are as quiet as they can be. Other groups like the drivers to make a lot of noise. I believe that a noisy drive gets more deer moving, but they are moving faster when they pass the standers.

Drooling

During the rutting season, all males of the deer family drool drops or strings of saliva. The more sexually excited the male becomes, the more it drools. I figure that a white-tailed buck may drool as much as 1½ quarts of saliva a day.

Droppings

Another word for the feces of the deer. Scat and manure are synonyms.

Deer droppings or scat.

Drug immobilization

More research has probably been done on the white-tailed deer than on any other big game animal. Because of this, our knowledge of this fantastic animal is growing constantly. Much of the research is done by the use of collared individuals. The deer are usually captured by the use of a dart containing an immobilization drug. While the deer is unconscious, the collar is placed on the neck and blood samples are taken. Everyone must work quickly as the drug's effectiveness is short-term, and in twenty minutes or so, the deer has recovered enough to scramble to its feet and run off.

Dry firing

Dry firing is pulling the trigger on your firearm without having a live round in the chamber. You should not allow the hammer to fall on a firing pin without having something for the pin to hit or the pin may break. There are special dry firing casings available for all types of firearms. If nothing else, use a fired casing. When dry firing, never point at anything but a target, just to be safe.

Ducks Unlimited

Ducks Unlimited (DU) is an international organization of sportsmen from Mexico, Canada, and the United States. It is one of the oldest and most successful conservation organizations and has greatly aided the comeback that waterfowl have made in the past 50 years. They have raised hundreds of millions of dollars to buy and lease land, create marshes and other habitat, monitor waterfowl populations, maintain research laboratories, and so on. DU is based in Memphis, Tennessee, at One Waterfowl Way, Memphis, TN 38120; phone 901-758-3825; fax 901-758-3850; www.ducks.org.

Dynamics

When used with wildlife, dynamics is usually a study of the animal's population. With deer, the study is concerned with statistics such as the deer's actual numbers in relation to their habitat, the age composition of the herd, the recruitment rate of fawns born to the actual number joining the herd as adults, the mortality rate, and so on.

E

Ear curl

When the tips of a fawn's ears curl backward on fawns that are being bottle-fed, it is a sign of dehydration. It is also a sign that a fawn found in the wild may be orphaned. Either the fawn is not getting enough liquid intake or is losing excessive liquid through diarrhea. Giving the fawn Pedialyte will stop the diarrhea and give it the needed electrolytes.

Eastern elk (*C. e. canadensis*)

This elk is extinct, having been wiped out by hunters from all of the eastern United States by the late 1800s. Elk have been brought back to a number of eastern states, but they are Rocky Mountain elk.

Eastern moose (*A. a. americana*)

The eastern moose is also known as the taiga moose. Its range is the boreal forests from Newfoundland, Canada, to a line from

The eastern moose are increasing in the New England states.

Lake Superior north to James Bay. This subspecies of moose is greatly expanding both its population and range, having spread from Maine throughout New England and into New York.

Economic factors

The cost involved with, or resulting from, something is the economic factor. The cost involved even affects deer management. For example, according to the Insurance Information Institute, deer are now responsible for more than 500,000 deer/vehicle collisions in the United States each year. The damage to vehicles costs one billion dollars to repair. Over 200,000 people are injured annually and more than 200 killed, a cost that can't be calculated. To reduce deer/car accidents, many states have liberalized their hunting seasons to reduce the deer population.

Edge

Edges are one of the most important habitat features. Edge is where a forest meets a field, where a field meets a road, where

Clear-cutting under power lines creates both edges and good deer browse.

two different types of habitat abut one another. Edges are important because they usually have a wide diversity of vegetation, producing good food and cover for many species of wildlife.

Ejaculation

The releasing of the seminal fluid and sperm from the male's testicles, via the penis, through masturbation, copulation, or electrical stimulation, which is being used in artificial insemination programs.

Emergency blankets

Every hunter should carry an emergency space blanket, available in most sporting goods stores. These highly reflective blankets are about the size of a granola bar and fit easily in your pocket. In emergencies, you can wrap up in the blanket or use it as a tent, and the reflective properties will prevent the loss of your body heat.

Emergent vegetation

The first vegetation that sprouts in the spring, and the first vegetation to rise above the water's surface, is known as emergent vegetation.

Endemic

A species that is native to a particular place. The white-tailed deer is not endemic to New Zealand; it had to be introduced.

Endocrine system

Endo is from the Greek language and means inside. The glands of the endocrine system empty their secretions directly into the body's bloodstream, where they are carried to the designated cells. The pineal, pituitary, adrenal, testes, and others are the glands that control everything that deer do and when they do it.

Energy expenditure

The body expends energy for such normal functions as the heart beating to circulate blood, the lungs expanding, and the digestion of food. Those are involuntary expenditures. Any activity, such as walking and running, is a voluntary expenditure, even when the creature doesn't want to do them. It is exceedingly important not to disturb deer during the winter months, when they will have to expend energy to get away at a time when they have little food and can't replace the calories expended.

Bounding in deep snow causes a deer to expend a tremendous amount of energy.

Epidermal cap

The very tip of the growing antler that is sheathed in velvet has an epidermal cap at the site where the minerals that form the antler are being laid down.

Epithelium

The layer of cells forming the tissue that makes up the outer layer of skin. With deer, it is used most frequently to describe the inside lining of the nostrils and mouth.

Epizootic hemorrhagic disease

An epizootic is a disease which appears temporarily, although annually. The outbreak runs its course and then stops. EHD, as this disease is known, occurs annually in some parts of the country. It can be devastatingly deadly to white-tailed deer and is usually the result of overpopulation. There are two types of EHD viruses and five types of blue tongue. The symptoms of all seven are identical. The animals lose body fluids directly through their tissue (hemorrhaging), they develop a blue tongue, and they often seek out water while they can still move. The viruses are spread by biting midges and the disease is usually arrested when frost kills off the midges. See *Blue tongue.*

Erector pili muscles

Beneath the skin of animals and birds is a layer of muscles that can cause the hair covering on animals to stand on end and allows birds to fluff their feathers. They may do this voluntarily to ward off the cold or it may be an involuntary action in response to fear.

Erosion

Where deer are overpopulated in hilly country, they can be the cause of extensive erosion. When the deer overbrowse an area to the point that they denude the area of all, or most, of the ground cover, hard rains will then cause the soil to erode. As deer are creatures of habit, they tend to use the same trails constantly. When these trails go up over a hill, the vegetation is often killed and the trails become channels for the run-off water, causing erosion.

Esophagus

The esophagus is a tube that starts below the pharynx and delivers food to the stomach.

Estrus cycle

The estrus cycle in deer, elk, and the rest of the deer family is the period when the female can be made pregnant. It is governed by photoperiodism, which keys the actual time of conception so that the gestation period timing causes the young to be born at the optimal time in the spring. Hormones produced 24 to 48 hours before the peak of the cycle

During the cow's estrus period, the bull elk will be with her constantly. Credit: Irene Vandermolen

cause the females to become agitated and to seek out the males. This period is known as pre-estrus. The actual estrus period lasts 26 to 28 hours, during which the female ovulates, discharging eggs from her ovaries into her uterus where they can be fertilized if she is bred by the male. If the female does not breed, or does not conceive, she goes out of estrus but comes back into the cycle approximately 28 days later. White-tailed does are known to have as many as seven estrus cycles per year.

European elk

The European counterpart to the North American elk is the red deer, which is often referred to as the European elk. To make the situation more confusing, the European moose is also referred to as an elk. The German word for moose is *elch,* the Swedish word is *ailg.*

Excitation jump

Caribou, when excited or frightened, will frequently rear up on their hind legs, jump to one side or the other, and make a jump as they start to trot off. The splaying of their hooves causes interdigital gland scent to be deposited on the tundra to serve as a warning of possible danger to other caribou that pass that way later.

Exocrene glands

Exo from the Greek means outside; these are glands that exit their secretions from the body. The best-known of these glands for the deer family are the tarsal, metatarsal, preorbital, forehead, salivary, and interdigital glands.

Exploitive competition

Mule deer are now scarce in Yellowstone National Park since the elk herd population has grown so large. The fact that the elk, because of their much larger size, can reach vegetation so much higher than the mule deer is an example of exploitive competition.

Extirpate

To wipe out a species completely. The eastern elk were completely annihilated by overhunting.

Eye aversion

Not making direct eye contact. A subordinate animal usually avoids looking directly at a dominant animal to show its submission.

Eye shine

The retina, the receptive surface at the back of the eye, is composed of rod and cone cells. Behind the rod cells in

The tapetum at the rear of a deer's eye reflects the "eye shine" we see when a light is shined at the deer.

many animals, including deer, is a reflective layer known as the tapetum, which passes the light back through the rods, doubling the amount of light the optic nerves receive. This produces the "eye shine" for which deer are famous. It has been calculated that deer can see at least one thousand times better than humans in low-light situations.

Eye tine

The first point or tine on the inside of a deer's antler is known as the eye or brow tine and is designated as the G-1 tine.

This white-tailed buck has unique palmated eye, or brow, tines.

F

Face mask

The use of a face mask is not as important in gun hunting as it is in bow hunting unless you are stalking, because usually the deer are being pushed and have less opportunity to see you. I prefer a face mask over face camouflage because it is less messy and quicker to use. The reflectancy of a human face is high and a dead giveaway to deer.

Fair chase

Any hunter wishing to register his trophy animal with the Boone & Crockett Club must certify that the animal was taken by fair chase. The Boone & Crockett rules are as follows:

Fair Chase Statement for All Hunter-Taken Trophies:

To make use of the following methods shall be deemed as Unfair Chase and unsportsmanlike, and any trophy obtained by use of such means is disqualified from entry for Awards.

  I. Spotting or herding game from the air, followed by landing in its vicinity for pursuit.
 II. Herding or pursuing game with motor-powered vehicles.
III. Use of electronic communications for attracting, locating, or observing game, or guiding the hunter to such game.
IV. Hunting game confined by artificial barriers, including escape-proof fencing; or hunting game transplanted solely for the purpose of commercial shooting.

Fanny pack

A fanny pack is a small belt pack worn around the waist. It is usually large enough to carry your lunch, thermos, and, perhaps, a "point-and-shoot" camera.

In winter, deer eat less and remain bedded as much as they can to conserve energy.

Fasting metabolism

As a survival tactic, all members of the deer and bovine families experience a slowing down of the basal metabolic rate each winter. It usually starts around the first of December and lasts until about the first of March. Latitude accounts for the actual timing. During the winter months, food for all animals in the wild is minimal. By slowing their metabolism, animals need less food and use their body fat much more slowly. In fact, once their metabolism slows, the animals could not eat more if it was available. I have found that a deer's intake is reduced by 50 to 60 percent of what it would normally eat.

Fawn

The young of the white-tailed, black-tailed, and mule deer are called fawns. On rare occasion, caribou calves are referred to as fawns.

A black-tailed doe and fawn.

Fawn camouflage

It is a well-known fact that fawns have a russet-red coat with white spots. This is to allow the fawn to blend in with small shafts of sunlight that shine through to the fallen leaves on the forest floor. See *Cryptic coloration.*

Feces

Excrement, manure, scat, droppings, and feces are just some of the words that are used to refer to the waste products excreted by animals. The feces of the deer family vary in consistency according to the animal's diet. When eating grass and other soft food, the feces are often a soft, formless mass. When feeding on browse and more ligneous material, the feces are compacted tightly into separate pellets of different shapes. These are often called fecal pellets.

Fecundity

Fecundity refers to how fertile or productive a female of the species is. Whitetails are considered more fecund than moose because a doe will usually produce twin fawns and, occasionally, on very nutritious food, triplets or quadruplets. A cow moose usually produces a single calf and occasionally twins. Because deer are more fecund than moose, their population grows much faster.

Fee hunting

As our human population continues to grow, an ever-increasing problem for many hunters is finding a place to hunt. In many cases, individuals, or a club to which they belong, will lease the hunting rights to a piece of property. Many people now go to a commercial hunting club and pay for the lodging and the right to shoot one of the animals.

Feeding areas

A deer feeding area is wherever food is currently available. The deer know where every fruit tree in their area is and when the fruit drops. They know the berry patches. They know when and where the farm crops are. They know where all the oak and beechnut trees are and when the nuts drop. If you want to know where a deer's feeding areas are, know where the food is.

Feeding deer

Feeding deer should only be done if it is necessary to save a herd from extinction during extreme circumstances. Ordinarily deer only need to be fed when the population has grown so large that they are destroying their range. By feeding starving deer, more will survive and the habitat will suffer further damage. The proper course of action is to reduce the number of deer in the area, by regulated sport hunting, before the habitat has been ruined. It takes years for a devastated habitat to recover.

Feral dogs

Feral dogs are dogs that have been abandoned or that have gone wild. They are a major threat to wildlife of all kinds and often to people as well. In northern areas, they wreak havoc on deer herds during the winter.

A young white-tailed deer that has been attacked by feral dogs and had its hind legs torn.

Fetus

The developing, unborn young of mammals.

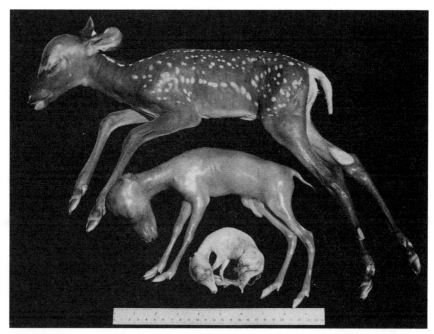

Sixty-day, 120-day, and 180-day fetuses.

Field dressing

To get the finest-quality meat from an animal that is shot, it is imperative that the hunter remove the viscera (i.e., guts) from the animal as soon as possible. If a deer is field-dressed, the skin on its body is opened and its paunch, intestines, bladder, and reproductive organs are taken out. The liver, heart, and lungs are left in and the diaphragm is left intact to help hold these organs in place and keep the chest area clean.

Fifth tine

The fifth tine is the fifth point projecting from the main beam of the antler. In deer or elk, this tine or point is also known as the G-5.

Fighting

Fighting between the males of the deer family does not occur as often as most folks believe. Males that have been in fraternal groups have usually established the dominance hierarchy, and their place in it, by social sparring before the rut actually takes place. Fights most often take place when two equal animals meet that have not met before. If neither backs down after the display of body language, a fight to prove dominance may occur. Only equal animals fight.

A vicious fight between two large white-tailed bucks.

Fire starters

Anyone who plans to be out in the winter woods should have the means to light a fire, because a fire may save your life. The most reliable method is to have a match safe that is watertight. There are good plastic ones available for about one dollar. I have carried a brass "Marble" match safe for over 50 years.

A handy survival item that will allow you to start a fire in almost any weather is one of the many types of fire starters that are available in any sporting goods shop. Many of the starters are paraffin-based. All of them light easily and last for a considerable time. Lacking a fancy fire starter, you can carry a short candle, which will work almost as well and costs just a fraction of the starter.

Make sure you fill the match safe with "strike anywhere" blue-tip matches. Some wooden matches can only be lit by striking a special surface. Cigarette lighters work very well, but the fuel will evaporate over time. Propane lighters are good if the weather does not get too cold. In cold weather, propane lighters don't light. Wooden kitchen matches are cheapest and best.

Fire suppression

The summer of the year 2000 saw the western forests devastated by the worst forest fires in history. The drought exacerbated the conditions. However, the main contributing factor was that the government, for years, quickly put out every little fire as soon as it started. Because of the strict fire suppression, the burnable material continued to accumulate over the years. Under natural conditions, smaller, less-destructive fires would have occurred periodically and would have prevented the excessive buildup of flammable material.

Flagging

When whitetails run off with their tails held high, we call it flagging. Does almost always flag when they run off because it allows their fawns to see and follow them better. Bucks sometimes run off with their tails up, but more often run off with their tails clamped down so as not to draw attention to themselves.

Flail

The females of all members of the deer family often stand erect on their hind feet and strike out, or flail, at their opponents with their forefeet. The males also do this in fighting after they have shed their antlers or when they don't want to injure their new, growing antlers.

Flehmen

A German word used to describe the lip-curling deep breathing that the male animals do to determine if the female is in estrus. The male breathes in the scent molecules deeply, raises his muzzle high, and curls his upper lip, which closes his nostrils, blocking the scent inside where it saturates the sensory nerve endings in the epithelial lining. While holding this position, he then exhales through his wide-open mouth, forcing some of the scent molecules past the vemeronasal organ.

Mule deer buck flehmening. Credit: Irene Vandermolen

A bull elk flehmening.

Flight or fight distance

All birds and animals have a distance beyond which they will not allow another creature to come before they will fly or run off. That is the flight distance, and it varies with the individual, the species, and the situation. A creature coming in closer than that invades the fight distance and may precipitate an attack by the original species, which now feels that its life is threatened. A creature may feel "cornered" in a wide-open space if it believes that you could catch it before it could get away.

Floating for deer

In wilderness areas, where it is possible to get a vehicle near a stream that can be floated, hunting from a canoe is a good method. Floating does not work in heavily hunted areas, because where pressure is high, the deer spend most of their time hiding in dense brush and will not be seen along the banks. Make sure that you can get your canoe out of the river and have someone meet you at a designated time so that you can get back up to your own vehicle that was left upstream.

Florida Key white-tailed deer (*O. v. clavium*)

This smallest subspecies of the whitetail is found in North America. It is found only in the Florida Keys and is on the endangered species list, as its population is down to about 300 to 350 animals. The greatest threat to its existence is the heavy automobile traffic in the Florida Keys.

A fine Florida Key white-tailed deer buck.

Florida white-tailed deer (*O. v. seminolus*)

This is a good-sized deer with a good rack. Some of the Florida deer that I photographed in the Okeefenokee Swamp in Georgia were every bit as large as those I have photographed in my home state of New Jersey. This subspecies is the deer of the Everglades.

Flukes

Flukes are parasitic flatworms that are sometimes seen in deer livers. The cysts are usually one to two inches across and appear yellowish. The deer can tolerate the flukes in low numbers, but they may become anemic with a heavy infestation. Deer livers infected with flukes should not be eaten, although the meat can be eaten. The flukes pose no health hazard to humans.

Food studies

Food studies are done to ascertain what foods the various species eat. Because there are no pristine areas left, I believe all food studies may be flawed. In the case of watching to see what a deer eats, it must be understood that the deer is picking from among the vegetation that is available. What the deer seems to prefer may be what is now found in that particular area. The deer's actually preferred food may have all been eaten a long time ago by the deer that lived there previously.

Foot stamping

Foot stamping is a sign of extreme nervousness in deer. It is done more frequently by whitetails than by mule or black-tailed deer. Although it is done by both sexes, it occurs more frequently among does. The deer may stand in one spot and stamp just one foot repeatedly or it may alternate its feet. Occasionally the deer will actually walk toward whatever arouses its suspicion, trying to identify it. At times the deer will stamp its feet alternately as it circles to try to get the scent of the potential danger. In stamping its feet, the deer is advertising the fact that it is fully alert and will not be surprised. It is also warning other deer of the potential danger; they can hear the stamping and feel the vibrations through the earth. When they stamp their feet, scent from their inter-

A nervous Texas white-tailed doe stamping its forefoot.

digital glands is deposited on the ground, and this serves to alert any deer that pass that way at a later time.

Forage

The vegetative material that the members of the deer family eat is known by the overall term of forage, whether the material is grasses, browse, or lichens.

Foraging patterns

All animals have different methods of obtaining the food they eat. Deer feed much more selectively than do elk and moose, which, being much larger, feed upon more species of coarser vegetation. Deer seldom stay in one spot for a minute while feeding. They take a bite here and a bite there, moving slowly all the time. Caribou, in migration, snatch mouthfuls of food on the run, actually a fast walk or trot. Moose will stand and strip the leaves from an entire clump of willows before moving on. Elk mow the grasses in semicircles as they walk slowly.

Forbs

Most of the broadleafed plants are known as forbs to differentiate between them and the narrow-bladed grasses. Deer prefer forbs over grass.

Forehead glands

All of the deer, both bucks and does, have sudoriferous glands in their forehead skin, with the male having many more than the female. The glands are found from just above the eyes to the base of the ears. These glands are rather quiescent during the summertime, but increase in size and glandular output with the advent of the rutting season. The more dominant the male, the more active his glands will be and the darker his skullcap will be stained. Bucks frequently rub scent from their glands on saplings and then lick it off, showing that it is as attractive to themselves as it is to all other deer.

Forest openings

Openings in mature forest may be made by humans clear-cutting the area, by fire, or by disease. Any forest opening will soon have a regrowth of very nutritious deer food. The Indians practiced game management long before Europeans came to North America. They would set fire to tracts of virgin forest near their villages because they knew it would attract the deer, and they would not have to go far to secure them.

Forkhorn

A term usually applied to the antlers of a young buck that has just four points or tines; a forked set of antlers.

A four-point, or forkhorn, white-tailed buck.

Fragmentation of habitat

Deer actually thrive better when larger forested areas are fragmented or broken up. Moose need larger unbroken blocks of forest, although they too need the food regeneration that occurs in clear-cuts. What is most devastating to the animals is when urbanization or other human activities prevent their traditional travel or migration routes from being used, when their wintering and yarding areas are destroyed, or when their habitat is so fragmented that the animals can't use what pieces are left.

Fraternal groups

The males of all members of the deer family keep themselves separate from the females except during the breeding season or when they are forced to spend the winter together as a protection from the weather or to have access to food.

In migration, elk and caribou bulls will travel in separate groups and at different times than the females. According to the species and the situation, the males may gather in large or small fraternal or bachelor groups.

Free-ranging

Animals that live in the wild under natural conditions.

Frontal skull plate

The skulls of the deer family have two large frontal bones running from the nasal bones in the front to the occipital bones in the rear. The antler pedicels grow out of, and across part of, the rear of the two frontal skull plates.

Funnels

Hunters should know where every funnel is in the area they hunt because the wildlife know and use them. There are many natural funnels, such as gaps between mountains, creek beds, narrowed strips of land between ponds and lakes, and other natural corridors. There are many more human-made funnels, such as barways or gateways in fences, tapered woodlots, brushy fencerows, and passageways around buildings.

Gaits

The different methods of forward motion of the deer are walking, trotting, and galloping. The mule deer has a unique gait known as stotting.

A black-tailed doe trotting.

Gambrel

A wooden or metal piece of equipment that is inserted behind the tendons on the hind legs of deer, elk, and other large game and used to hold them up so they can be skinned and butchered.

Game warden

Game wardens and their deputies, conservation officers, or environmental protection officers are just a few of the names used to describe the men and women who risk their lives to protect wildlife and to enforce the game laws of their respective states. For many of these officers today, their role is as much education as it is enforcement. Hunters everywhere owe a debt of gratitude to these officials, who are in large part responsible for the fantastic hunting opportunities most of us enjoy today.

Gamey taste

The meat of any of the Cervidae does not, in itself, have a "gamey" taste. The so-called gamey taste is the result of the inept handling of the carcass by the hunter. The hunter may break the deer's bladder and pour the urine on the hams. He may handle the tarsal glands and transfer the musky odor to the meat. He may not eviscerate the animal properly and may spill the contents of the paunch inside the carcass. He may not eviscerate the animal as soon as it is down, allowing for a gas buildup in the internal organs. He may not remove the popliteal and prescapular glands, which will impart a bad taste to the meat. Proper handling means good meat.

Gasset, José Ortega y

A Spanish nobleman and a famed hunter, who wrote in his classic book, *Meditations on Hunting,* in 1942: "One does not hunt in order to kill. On the contrary, one kills in order to have hunted."

Gauge

Shotgun gauges are figured on how many balls it takes to make a pound. The 28-gauge takes 28; the 20, 16, 12, and 10 all take the number designated to the gauge. The exception is the .410, which is 410/1000 of an inch like a rifle caliber. This allowed the old .45-caliber pistol shells to be used in it.

Genes

Genes are the basic code of heredity containing DNA that are a part of the chromosomes contributed by each of the parents. Together, these make up the individual.

Giardia lamblia

Sometimes called beaver fever, this parasite is picked up by drinking untreated water. It causes severe diarrhea in humans. The beaver is a known host and the moose is also suggested to be one. Filtering water removes the cysts; this should be done before drinking.

Gibbous

A term most hunters would not encounter outside the "phase of the moon" hunting strategies becoming so popular. Gibbous means when a sphere is more than half illuminated, but not yet fully. It applies to the phase when the moon is ¾ full, either waxing or waning.

Girdled trees

Removing the bark from a sapling all around the trunk is known as girdling, and the tree usually dies. All members of the deer family may girdle saplings by rubbing them with their antlers. Moose and elk often girdle trees by peeling off the bark with their teeth when eating.

Glassing

The telephone companies used to have a slogan, "Let your fingers do the walking," meaning just leaf through their directory for the service you desire. In hunting, especially on the open Western plains or in mountainous regions, your slogan should be, "Let your eyes do the walking." In other words, select a vantage point and then use good binoculars or a spotting scope to look for game at a distance. In the field, I live with a small pair of Steiner Rocky 10×28 binoculars around my neck. Hunters can use larger binoculars because they will not have the heavy camera gear I usually carry. In my opinion, 8×40 field binoculars are an excellent choice for deer hunters.

The big advantage to glassing for game is that you can look around while sitting still. Most big game has vision that

Pine tree with bark rubbed off by moose antlers.

is perhaps six to eight times better than human eyesight. If we are moving about, there is a good chance the game will see us first and be gone.

Gloger's Rule

Gloger's Rule states that, among warm-blooded animals, dark pigments are most prevalent in warm, humid habitats. I must add that dark coloration also tends to prevail in even the northern forested areas.

Gnawed antlers

We all need calcium for strong bones. We need more calcium as we get older to prevent osteoporosis; wildlife does also. Wildlife instinctively knows it can get the needed calcium by gnawing or chewing on bones and antlers, and all rodents and members of the canine and feline families chew on them when they can find them. Cervidae occasionally will chew on shed antlers, but they get most of their calcium from the vegetation they eat or from mineral licks.

Gonadatrophic hormones

Gonad is another word for testicles. Trophic means to nourish. The activities of all members of the deer family are governed

Antlers gnawed by rodents.

by photoperiodism. As the days begin to shorten in July and August, the pineal gland picks up a little less light each day. This, in turn, stimulates the pituitary gland, located at the base of the brain, to produce a gonadatrophic luteinizing hormone that causes the testicles of the buck to enlarge, which in turn increases the production of testosterone. This causes the antlers to solidify and starts the entire pre-rut activity.

GPS system

The global positioning system was developed by our government for the armed forces. There are a number of satellites in space that rotate with the earth. By using a GPS handheld receiver, you can get your exact position to within 50 feet or so. By recording the location of your car or camp before you start out, you can hunt all day and the receiver will tell you where you are and how to get back to your starting point.

Graze

An animal that grazes is one that eats grasses and forbs.

Green-up

Green-up occurs each spring when the ambient temperature reaches about 40 degrees Fahrenheit, which warms up the earth enough to allow the first green vegetation to sprout.

Ground blinds

Most bow hunters use tree stands; most gun hunters hunt from the ground. To increase your chances of success on the ground, a blind is a big help. It can range from something as simple as camouflaged cloth strung up on sticks so the outline of the hunter is minimized to commercial pop-up blinds resembling little tents. The drawback to the pop-ups is that they restrict vision and movement, but they do keep the hunter warmer in extremely cold weather.

Grunt tube

A cylinder of either plastic or wood containing a vibrating reed that when blown produces a sound like a buck grunting.

Grunting

The low-pitched, raspy sound that bucks make, primarily during the rutting season. It is the sound that hunters try to imitate when using a grunt tube.

Guard hair

Most mammals have two layers of hair. The stiff, water-repellent, long, outer hairs and the softer, woolly undercoat. The guard hairs of the members of the deer family are hollow in the center, which allows those hairs to provide good insulation. A whitetail has 2,600 guard hairs to the square inch in its winter coat. The long, hollow guard hairs of a

Summer deer hair on left, winter coat in center, winter coat with woolly undercoat on right. Note how much larger the guard hair is in winter than in summer.

caribou's winter coat makes it one of the warmest coats of all animals. It also provides the caribou with exceptional buoyancy, allowing their bodies to float high in the water when they swim.

Gun fit

To shoot a gun that "fits" is a joy. To shoot a gun that doesn't fit means you will not shoot well at all. As we all have different body shapes, arm lengths, and so on, it stands to reason that a mass-produced gun will never fit as well as one that has a customized stock made to fit just you. When you pull a gun up to your shoulder and your cheek snugs down to the comb and the front and rear sights line up perfectly so you really don't have to see them, that gun fits. If that's not what your gun feels like, you can file down the comb or build it up, you can shorten the stock, or you can add a shooting pad or extender. There are many things you can do for yourself or that your local gunsmith can do for you. A gun that doesn't fit is an abomination.

Gun sights

There are many different types of iron gun sights that are still being used today. Many scope sighted rifles have high mounts that allow their iron sights to be used in poor light conditions or where the action is very fast. Some of the rear sights are flat with a V cut in, and some are curved on each side of the V and are known as "buckhorn" sights. A peep sight is a disc with small holes in the center. Often the disc is on a tang or post to raise the sight higher. Iron front sights are usually a blade or a bead on a post.

Habitat

The area in which a creature lives. It is considered good habitat if it provides food, water, and cover suitable to the species' needs.

Handgun

A general name for any of the short-barreled guns that are fired while supported with one or two hands. Occasionally a handgun will be fitted with a shoulder stock that allows for greater accuracy. A single-shot pistol, a revolving cylinder pistol, and a semi-automatic pistol are all types of handguns.

Head bobbing

Caribou calves alone among the North American Cervidae are followers instead of hiders. To encourage their calves to follow them, and to imprint on them, the female caribou face their calves as soon as the calves can stand and bob their heads up and down in a vertical fashion. When the calves respond, the mother licks the calf and allows it to nurse. Then she moves off, faces her calf again and bobs her head. The reward of nursing soon has the calf following its mother as the herd moves on.

Heart rate

The basic heart rate is figured when a creature is at rest. Activity, anger, fear, or other emotions all speed up the heart rate in anticipation of whatever action is to be taken.

Herbivore

Animals that eat primarily grasses or woody vegetation, like all members of the deer family, are classified as herbivores.

Herding

Elk and caribou form harems of cows, while mule deer and moose may occasionally gather a few females together. The

Bull elk herding calf back to his harem. Credit: Len Clifford

white-tailed and black-tailed deer seek out just the female that is in estrus at the moment. The elk bull does the greatest amount of herding, pushing the cows ahead of him into the forest when he wants to bed down and pushing them out into the meadows when it is time to feed. In the herding posture, the bull lays his antlers back along his body and circles the herd to keep them together or to direct which way he wants them to go. Cows that refuse or are slow to respond may be gored with his antlers.

Hierarchy

The status, or ranking, of a creature on the scale of dominance is the hierarchy or pecking order. The number one animal or bird is dominant over all of the others. The number two animal is subordinate to number one, but dominant over all the others, and so on, down to the creature that everyone dominates.

Highlining

When deer and elk become overpopulated, they consume all of the vegetation that they can reach, even standing on their hind feet to do so. When they do this, they are said to be highlining or creating a browse line.

Hilton Head white-tailed deer (*O. v. hiltonenses*)

This subspecies of the whitetail is found only on Hilton Head Island off the coast of South Carolina.

Hind

The female of the European red deer, the counterpart of North American elk, is referred to as a hind.

Historically

When you read of an account about wildlife and it refers to "historically," the writer is referring to any time since the coming of the Europeans to this continent in 1492. Prior to that time is referred to pre-Columbian. Since the native Indians did not have a written language, it was not until the Europeans arrived that historical records could be accurately kept.

Hock gland

A common name for the tarsal gland, located at the juncture of the tarsus and tuber calsis bones, the area corresponding to our ankle. It is the most important scent gland of the deer. See *Tarsal gland.*

Home range

No member of the deer family actually has a territory except deer does during their birthing period. They have home ranges, the areas they inhabit during the year. For the whitetail, the home range is one to two square miles. During the

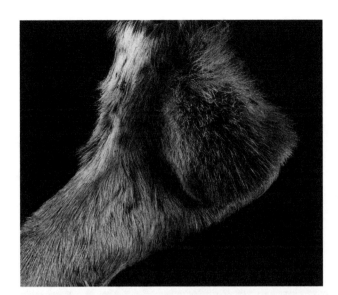

A whitetail's hock, or tarsal, gland.

rutting season, bucks will expand their range up to about eight to ten square miles. Most of the species have a winter and a summer home range. See *Territory.*

Homeothermic

Warm-blooded. Homeothermic means that deer are able to maintain an average body temperature of about 101 degrees Fahrenheit, no matter what the ambient temperature might be. However, maintaining that body temperature when the ambient temperature is very low comes at a high caloric cost. The deer, being unable to eat more, must utilize its fat reserves to produce enough energy to stay warm.

Hoof

Our fingernails and the deer's hooves are composed of keratin, which is a fibrous protein that hardens. While the basal part is living material, the distal portion dies.

The massive horns of a bighorn ram. Credit: Len Rue, Jr.

Horns

Deer do not have horns, they have antlers. Horns are found on sheep, goats, cattle, bison, and antelope. Horns have a central core of living material; the outer layer keratinizes or dies, just as fingernails do.

Hot Hands

Handwarmers, such as Hot Hands, are chemical packets that, when crushed or shaken, will provide heat for eight to 12 hours. They can be placed in your mittens, tucked along your legs in your boots, placed under your belt in the small of your back, or carried in your pocket. I place them next to my photographic equipment in bitterly cold weather to keep my cameras operating. They can be purchased from the L.L. Rue catalog by calling 800-734-2568.

Hummel

This is a European term that describes a red deer stag that is too old to grow antlers. It is sometimes used to describe old bull moose.

Hunter education program

This program is mandatory in almost all of the states before hunting licenses can be obtained. The courses vary from state to state, but they include instruction in safe gun and bow hunting, a knowledge of the game laws, discussion of the courtesy toward landowners and other hunters, and sometimes the care and preparation of the meat. This program and the wearing of blaze-orange apparel have greatly reduced hunting accidents across the nation.

Hunter's ear

The Hunter's Ear is a hearing aid device designed to be used by anyone who wants to hear better under any circumstances. Even if you have perfect hearing, the Ear lets you hear deer coming at an even greater distance so you are prepared before the deer get to you. A big advantage the Ear has over regular hearing aids is that it protects your hearing by automatically shutting off all sound when you shoot. Information for the Hunter's Ear can be gotten from Bob Walker, P. O. Box 1069, Media, PA 19063; telephone 610-565-8952.

Hunting camps

Going to a hunting camp to get together with a group of your buddies was almost as important to tradition as were the deer. Someone in the group was usually a good cook or, if you didn't think the cooking was that great and complained, you became the cook. Youngsters were taken to camp and taught the fundamentals of deer hunting by the older men. Friendships were formed that lasted a lifetime. There was usually an acknowledged leader who supervised the strategy of the hunt, the placement of the standers, the direction of the drivers, and the division of the meat of the animals taken. There was a lot of good-natured ribbing and you lost your shirttail if you missed a shot at a buck. There were all-night card games and, at times, a little too much drinking, but only in the evening. Most camps were located in remote areas, at least areas that were remote at that time, as it was harder to travel 50, 75, and 100 years ago.

There are still hunting camps; the traditions are still carried out, but they are becoming few and far between. Most of us don't have the time to take a week off during the deer season. Travel has gotten so that most hunters can drive to their favorite hunting spots and get there before dawn. In most areas, deer are so plentiful that no one needs to go to remote areas to hunt.

Hunting Island white-tailed deer (*O. v. venatorius*)

This subspecies of the whitetail is found only on Hunting Island, South Carolina.

Hunting license

Almost all states require residents and non-residents to purchase a license before being allowed to hunt. Some states allow landowners to hunt their own land without a license. Most states require the hunter to complete a safety course before a first license will be issued. Most states require the hunter to have the license clearly displayed while hunting.

Hunting population

According to the statistics of almost every state, the number of hunters hunting deer is gradually, but steadily, declining. This is basically because most folks no longer live on family farms as they did a century ago. Although our population is constantly growing, most people no longer have their "roots in the soil." Folks living in urban or city areas are less inclined to hunt.

Hunting also becomes more difficult as more woodlands and farmlands are taken over by suburbia; it's just harder to find a place to hunt without traveling a considerable distance. In many areas, the only way to hunt is to join a hunting club, and that can be expensive.

Hunting with dogs

Although many hunters frown upon the use of dogs for driving deer, there are many areas where the deer just can't be moved without dogs. The extensive swamps in the southeastern United States or the cedar swamps in Ontario, Canada, are all but impassable by humans. Even using dogs does not guarantee that the deer will be moved past the standers. Many of the deer simply keep circling inside the swamps or lose the dogs by taking to the water.

J

Imprinting

One of the main reasons why does have a birthing territory is so that their fawns imprint on them instead of on another deer. A fawn has a tendency, right after being born, to follow, to imprint on, anything that moves near them, including humans. The tongue washing that the doe does to clean the fawn also helps to imprint her odor on the fawn as well as imprinting the fawn's odor on the doe. Does cannot recognize their fawns by voice; they do it by smell. Caribou cows imprint on their calves by head-bobbing, urging their young to follow them. They, too, have bonded by tongue washing.

A doe washes her newborn fawn to both clean and imprint it.

Incisor teeth

We humans have four incisor teeth, top and bottom, in the front of our mouths. Members of the deer family have six incisor teeth in the front of their mouths in the bottom jaw only. They have no teeth in the front of their mouths in the top jaw. They also have two pseudo incisor teeth in the lower jaw that are modified canine teeth, giving them eight teeth in the front of their mouths.

Infrared light

Infrared light has light waves that are beyond the wavelength of light visible to the human eye. There are night glasses available that enable us to view the heat radiating from an animal's body in the form of an image that can be seen.

Instinct

Any action or reaction that is taken without thought is said to be instinctive. All creatures have some, or most, of their responses as inborn or innate traits.

Intelligence

I, for one, do not believe that everything deer do is instinctive. I believe they are capable of cognition, capable of learning from experiences, capable of reaching new conclusions, and capable of thought. That said, let me also state that some deer are smarter than others, just as some humans are smarter than others. A major drawback for deer is that so many are shot before they have had a chance to gain the experience that would prove this intelligence.

Interdigital gland

Interdigital means between the toes. About two inches above a deer's two center hooves is a gland that has an opening varying in depth from 1 to 1½ inches. If you take a Q-tip and insert it in this gland, it will be coated with a grayish, waxy secretion that smells strongly of ammonia, much as the wax in

A whitetail's interdigital gland.

your ear does. This is the interdigital gland scent that deer deposit on the ground when they stamp their feet, which serves as a warning to other deer who encounter it later.

Intergrade

The boundaries that we humans have designated as separating the various subspecies of the deer family mean absolutely nothing to the animals. During the rutting season, the bucks or bulls breed any estrus female they can find. Where the ranges of two subspecies overlap and breeding takes place, it is said that the resultant offspring are intergrades.

Internet

Each state maintains a website on the Internet, and you can get that address from any source that sells hunting licenses. With a click of a mouse, you can find out about hunting seasons, license fees, game and fish laws and regulations, license sales, annual harvests, hunter success rates, and much more. There has never been so much data available so readily.

Interspecific

The relationship between different species of animals in a particular area. For example, how the wolves are affecting the elk population in Yellowstone National Park.

Intraspecific

The relationship between the animals of the same species in a particular area. For example, how the high browse line created by the bucks affects the survival of the fawns.

Inyo mule deer (*O. h. inyoensis*)

This deer has only a small range in and around Inyo County, California. In size and color, it is between the larger Rocky Mountain mule deer to the east and the smaller California mule deer to the west.

Ishi

The last surviving member of the Yana Indian tribe of the Lassen Peaks area of California. All of the rest of the tribe had been killed by the whites. Near starvation, he surrendered on August 25, 1911. Ishi was about 50 years of age at that time. Until his death on March 25, 1916, Ishi lived at the University of California Museum of Anthropology in San Francisco. While at the university, Ishi met Dr. Saxton Pope and taught him how to make bows and arrows and how to hunt with them. Ishi is owed a debt by all modern bow hunters. See *Pope & Young Club*.

Ivory

All teeth are basically ivory. However, the term ivory is usually applied to the two top canine teeth that are commonly found in elk and, occasionally, in white-tailed deer. These teeth serve no useful purpose; they are holdovers from prehistoric times and are in the process of being lost through evolution. There are no opposing canine teeth in the lower jaw.

There are four deer species—the musk, the tufted, the muntjac, and the Chinese water deer—that actually have small, saber-shaped tusks or elongated canine teeth.

ヲ

Jacobson's organ

Snakes wave their tongues in the air to pick up molecules of scent. The two tips to their tongues are then placed in the two openings of the Jacobson's organ, where the chemical molecules are changed to electrical impulses so that the snake's olfactory bulbs can identify the odor. This organ has its counterpart in the deer's vomeronasal organ, which performs the same duty. See *Vomeronasal organ.*

A timber rattlesnake flicks out its tongue to pick up scent molecules.

K

Kaibab plateau

Located in northern Arizona. It is used as a classic example of wildlife mismanagement. It was made into a preserve in 1906 and all predators were eliminated to help the mule deer herd. With no hunting and no predators, the herd grew from 3,000 deer to over 100,000 in 1923. By 1925, 30,000 to 60,000 deer died of starvation after the habitat was decimated. Between 1925 and 1930, 15,417 deer were shot or live-trapped. By 1931 the herd was down to 20,000. Through proper management, the habitat and the deer finally came back into balance.

Kansas white-tailed deer (*O. v. macrourus*)

This subspecies occurs in Texas, Oklahoma, Kansas, Nebraska, Iowa, Missouri, Arkansas, and Louisiana. It is a large deer with heavy main beams and short tines. The number one non-typical B&C whitetail head is of this subspecies.

Knives

The only time I don't have a knife on is when I don't have my pants on. I have carried a six-inch Randall sheath knife on the rear of my left hip for more than 50 years. You can skin a deer with a much smaller knife, but I can cut the ribs along the side of the sternum to open the rib cage with just one slash. There are many types and styles of knives designed for skinning, butchering, and many other uses. Never lay your knife down. Have it in your hand or in its sheath; then you won't lose it. My knife is a working tool that is an extension of my hand.

Koller, Larry

Larry Koller, who lived in Spring Valley, New York, was a famed outdoorsman, deer hunter, guide, and author. His book, *Shots at Whitetails,* is a timeless classic on hunting the white-tailed deer in the northeastern United States. His information on guns, ammunition, the whitetail itself, and hunting techniques are as applicable today as when the book was originally written in 1970.

Lacrimal gland

The gland located in front of the eye on members of the deer family is known as the preorbital, lacrimal, or tear duct gland. It is used in marking chemical signposts.

Lactation

The length of time that the females produce milk for their young is known as their lactation period. The young of the deer family are usually nursed about four months.

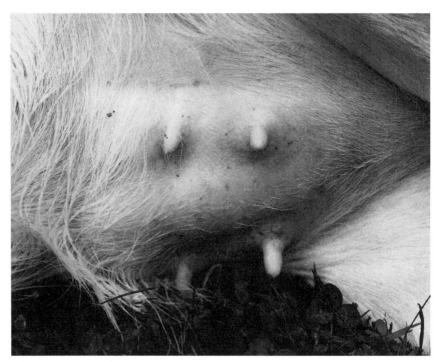

Before giving birth, the udders, or milk bags, of all cervids swell with milk.

Ladder stand

A folding ladder with a platform on top, on which a hunter can stand or sit while hunting. Most ladder stands are about 10 to 12 feet high and are favored by those who don't want to use a regular tree stand, yet want to be able to see over the surrounding brush.

Land use practices

No matter how the land is being used, whether it is being farmed, timbered, or lying fallow, it is known as the land use practices.

Latitude

There are 360 degrees to a circle or to the earth. The equator circling the midpoint of the earth is considered zero degrees latitude and the poles are 90 degrees. The lines running east and west on a map are called parallels of latitude. The tip of Florida is about 25 degrees north while the tip of Maine is about 57 degrees north, with all of the United States in between.

Layering

In cold weather, you will stay warmer wearing a number of light layers than one large bulky outfit because of the air trapped between the layers. Another advantage to layering is that you can dress lightly while you walk in to your stand, without perspiring, and then add extra layers after you cool down. Also, you can remove layers as you warm up.

Lead deer

Deer live in a matriarchal society, wherein the dominant doe is followed by at least two, and sometimes three, generations of females that are her blood-related family. All groups of the deer family are usually led by an old, smart female.

Lever-action rifle

Lever-action rifles are often preferred if they are to be carried on a horse because they have a flatter contour that fits well in a scabbard. More deer have probably been killed with a Winchester .30/30 lever-action rifle than with any other. With its short barrel, the gun can be handled quickly in dense brush, and the lever action is fast. A full stroke of the lever ejects the fired casing and pumps in a new cartridge from the tube as it cocks the external hammer. They are still used today, but have not been the gun of choice for deer hunting for at least 50 years.

Licking stick

I first discovered bucks using a licking stick around 1985. This is usually a resilient sapling of ½ to 1 inch in diameter that has been broken off about 30 to 36 inches above the ground. The bucks first rub the scent from their forehead glands on the stick and then lick it off. They particularly like to rub the stick on the glands behind their antlers and in front

White-tailed buck depositing forehead gland scent on a stiff weed.

Then he licks the scent off.

of their ears. I have no idea why they lick off the scent they have just deposited. These sticks are like magnets to all other deer, as every buck will add his scent and lick it off. I have even seen does lick off the scent, but I have not seen them rub their scent on the sticks. I have seen does rub their forehead scent on buck-rubbed saplings, though. Except for the fact that the top 6 to 8 inches of the licking stick have been rubbed bare, there is nothing to call your attention to it. I was the first to write about such sticks and have since seen hundreds of them. I'm sure you have seen them, too, but perhaps didn't know what you were seeing. Now you do.

Life span

The life span is the length of time that an animal can be expected to live. With deer, the life expectancy is 12 years; for caribou and elk it is about 15, and for moose it is 17 years. You must realize that, although some animals reach the expected age, the vast majority do not. Under normal condi-

The author with a 20-year-old white-tailed doe.

tions, the females of most species live longer than the males. Conversely, some animals, even in the wild, live much longer than their age span. There are records of wild white-tailed does living to be 22 years old.

Lignin

The woody portion of the cell walls of shrubs and trees that gives that type of vegetation its structural strength. Lignin, unlike the cellulose of plants, is not digestible. The cervids ingest the lignin when they eat woody vegetation, but derive no benefit from it. They can actually starve with their bellies full of woody material.

Line of sight

When you look over the gun sight, or through the scope of your gun, you look in a straight line at your target. This is your line of sight. However, your bullet does not travel in a straight line because it is dropping constantly after it leaves the barrel in response to the pull of gravity. While you are looking in a straight line, your bullet is traveling in an arc known as its trajectory. The bullet intersects with your line of sight twice, once about 25 feet from the barrel as it starts up the arc and again at the distance for which the gun is sighted, such as 100 yards. See *Trajectory.*

Lip curling

See *Flehmen.*

Lipogenesis

Lipids is another word for fat, and genesis means start. Lipogenesis is the buildup of fat on the body resulting from eating more food than is needed for daily body maintenance. Many birds and animals and some humans have to build up fat supplies on the body in order to survive the cold of winter. With wildlife, the fat buildup is the result of greater food consumption. With most humans, the fat buildup is also from overeating, although in many cases it is also caused by the person's genetic make-up or a glandular disturbance. It is in an animal's genes to get fat before winter; very few wild animals get fat from just overeating.

Live and dressed weights

As a rule of thumb, an animal loses 40 percent of its live weight after it has been eviscerated and bled out. I have found that, in addition, by removing all the bone, fat, and tissue, I get 48 pounds of pure meat from a 125-pound live deer.

Livestock

This is a term that applies to all of the different types of domesticated farm and ranch animals. It is not a term that is used to describe captive deer and elk because, although these animals are in captivity, they have not been domesticated.

Live-trapping

When our deer population was low, many states live-trapped deer where they were plentiful and moved them to areas that had no deer or very few deer. Many deer were shipped to different states in an effort to re-establish deer herds in areas from which they had been extirpated.

Live traps were usually made of wood, although some states used traps made of a pipe frame and netting. The traps were baited with apples, alfalfa hay, salt, corn, or anything else that was attractive to deer. Most trapping was done during the winter months when, because of food shortages, the deer were hungry and could more easily be enticed into a trap.

The cost of live-trapping and transporting a deer to another location runs $400 to $500 per deer. Very little live-trapping of deer is being done today because most areas have more deer than they have food to feed them. There are basically no more places to put deer.

A deer live trap.

Locked antlers

Basically, the antlers of all members of the deer family are shaped to catch an opponent's antlers squarely and to allow them to be disengaged easily when one of the animals realizes that his opponent is stronger. And that's what usually happens, but sometimes it doesn't. Rarely, when two rival males bang their antlers together with hundreds of pounds—and, in the case of moose, perhaps tons—of pressure, the antlers spring apart slightly and then spring back, securely locking the animals together. If the animals are not found and rescued by humans sawing one of the antlers off, the animals will both succumb and die of stress, dehydration, or starvation. There have been records of coyotes eating one of the locked deer that had died while the other deer was still alive. It must have been sheer terror for the survivor.

Great care must be taken by all persons trying to rescue bucks that have been locked together. There are records of the

Leonard Lee Rue III with locked Alaskan moose antlers.

freed buck trying to attack his rescuers. I know of two instances where three bucks locked their antlers together and died.

Long bow

This is the flat, traditional bow, measuring 5 to 6 feet in length, that has been in use for thousands of years. The taking of game with some of the compound bows, with their cams, levers, sights, and releases, has become so mechanical that many hunting purists are going back to the more challenging long bow.

Longitude

The lines, or meridians, running north and south on a map are the degrees of longitude. Greenwich, England, stands at zero degrees longitude. Greenwich is also the point at which each 24-hour day starts. Every 15 degrees of longitude represents one hour of time, in response to the earth's circumference of 24,000 miles. All lines of longitude go east or west of Greenwich.

Lordosis

This is the high, hump-back position often found in mutant deer. It is usually accompanied with short, bowed legs and bowed nasal bones.

Lumpy jaw

This is caused by a parasite, an arterial worm, called *Elaeophora schneideri.* The infection of this parasite causes a weakening in the tissue on the outside of the deer's lower jaw. In turn, this area becomes impacted with food that the deer eats, which gives it the very noticeable "lumpy jaw." The impaction often causes tooth loss, bone decay, and occasionally even death. Lumpy jaw is usually found only in old animals, as age weakens all creatures. It may occur in all of the cervids. It is spread from deer to deer by biting horseflies. It does not affect humans.

Lyme disease

Lyme disease is caused by a spirochete bacterium called *Borrelia burgdorferi.* It enters the human body when a person is bitten by an *Ixodes* tick and the spirochete enters the bloodstream. The hosts of the tick are deer, white-footed mice, over 40 species of birds, and probably any warm-blooded wild creature. The usual first signs of the infection, if you don't notice the tick, are flu-like symptoms and often a bull's-eye rash about three to four inches in diameter. If treated at once, the infection can easily be cured by oral antibiotics. If left untreated, there can be very serious results, such as neurological or cardiac problems. Lyme disease is now found in every state, and there have been well over 100,000 cases, with up to 20,000 new cases diagnosed each year. Prevention is the best cure. I spray my clothing with Permanone, a formula developed by the Armed Forces that kills the ticks. We list Permanone in the L.L. Rue catalog (800-734-2568).

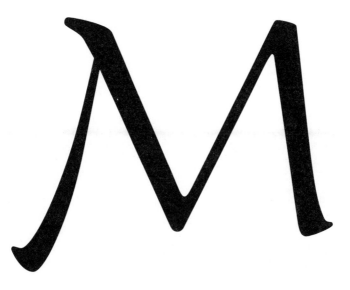

Madstone

See *Bezoar stone.*

Malnutrition

Malnutrition can be caused by either a general lack of food or a lack of highly nutritious food. In the case of wildlife, a deer may be getting enough food to sustain life, but only if it is getting sufficiently nutritious food will it be able to maximize its body and antler growth. In the all too many areas that are overpopulated with deer, the most nutritious foods, foods the deer favor, have long since been consumed and have been replaced by second- or even third-rate vegetation.

During a bad winter, many deer die of malnutrition.

Mandatory lipogenesis

Mandatory lipogenesis is a fancy term to describe the deer's need to fatten up in order to withstand the rigors of winter. Most hunters assume that the deer they shot is in good shape, that its range is in good condition, if they see fat in the deer's body. What they don't realize is that that fat has been accumulated on the deer's body at a cost to the deer's body growth. On good deer range, and that's not found in many areas, a deer will grow and gain body fat if it is getting sufficient nutritious food. On poor range, the deer will still accumulate some fat, but it will be a smaller deer. The deer in many forested areas of the country are producing smaller antlers and becoming smaller in stature due to overpopulation.

Mandible

The lower jaw in mammals and fish. Both the upper and lower parts of a bird's bill.

Mane

Stiff guard hairs on the top of a moose's neck and withers that grow to be six to eight inches in length. Piloerector muscles under the skin can cause these hairs to stand on end like a mane. It is a sign of extreme agitation, and when coupled with a lowered head and laid-back ears, it usually signifies that a charge is imminent.

Some deer actually do have a mane of longer hair located on the top of their necks. Like a true mane on horses and zebras, the mane cannot be erected.

Manitoban elk (*C. e. manitobensis*)

The elk found in the prairie provinces of Saskatchewan and Manitoba. These elk have a very limited range and are isolated by open prairies from the Rocky Mountain elk.

Market hunting

Today, the name market hunter is used to describe a rather unsavory character. It is true that overhunting did push many species of birds and animals to the brink of extinction. However, in their day, market hunters were highly respected individuals who filled a need by supplying wild game for those who could not take the game themselves. Wild game was thought to be an inexhaustible resource. We know today that it is not. We have the benefit of hindsight; the market hunters did not.

Masseter muscles

The large muscles fastened to the lower jaws of all of the mammals that bite and chew their food. They are especially well developed in all of the Cervidae to allow them to chew their cuds.

Mast

A common term used to describe a crop of nuts, berries, or fruit that falls from trees. The leaves of the trees, which the deer also eat, are not considered a mast crop.

Acorns are just one type of mast. Top left: blue oak; top right: valley oak; bottom right: coast black oak; and bottom left: interior live oak; all good black-tailed deer foods.

Masticating

An animal that is chewing its food is said to be masticating it. The term is used for animals that chew their food just one time before it is swallowed and digested, or, as in the case of ruminants, it is slightly chewed, swallowed, regurgitated, and then thoroughly chewed. In masticating its cud, the number of times an animal chews before the cud is reswallowed depends upon the toughness of the vegetation being chewed. White-tailed deer chew their cud about 45 times before it is swallowed. Mountain sheep and goats chew their cud about 80 times before reswallowing it.

Masturbation

Sexual self-gratification done by the male of most species of birds and animals; a way of relieving frustration. In the Cervi-

White-tailed buck masturbating.

dae, the males are capable of breeding from the last of August to the last of March. The females will accept a male's advances for only about 28 hours once a year. In masturbating, the Cervidae male usually balances on his front legs, extends his rigid penis beneath his brisket, and ejaculates after a few thrusts.

Maternal group

A maternal group is an all-female group, a matriarchy led by the oldest doe. In deer, the group is usually blood-related. This is not true of the elk and caribou, which form in actual herds.

Matriarchal group

See *Maternal group.*

Maturity

An animal is said to be mature when it has attained its full skeletal growth. The males of all of the members of the deer family reach this stage at about four years of age, the females at about two years. It is because of this time difference that there is such a size difference between the males and the females. It is because of the size difference that these animals are said to be dimorphic. It is only after the males have matured that they are capable of producing their very best antlers because food energy that had previously gone to body growth can now be diverted to antler growth. After maturity, the animals may grow heavier, but they do not grow larger.

Maximum sustained yield

For years, the basic goal in wildlife management was to produce the maximum number of huntable animals or birds, without destroying the habitat. Seasons and bag limits were adjusted on an annual basis. Food plantings were made to increase the land's carrying capacity. Today, the emphasis is not on the maximum number of a species the land will produce, but the maximum number that the public in general will tolerate.

Meatpole

A meatpole is a fixture at all hunting camps. It is used to hang the carcasses of harvested game as it is killed. If made properly, it gets the meat high enough to be beyond the reach of dogs. It is very difficult to hang meat beyond the reach of bears. In its simplest form, a meatpole is simply a trimmed sapling nailed horizontally between two trees.

Melanistic

A condition whereby the body produces a more than normal amount of melanin. When this occurs, animals have black hair and dark eyes instead of the normal color. This condition happens only occasionally in white-tailed deer.

Memory

Memory is being able to think about the past. All we humans really get out of life are memories. Memory in wildlife is often being able to benefit from past experiences without thinking about it, yet the action is a conscious action or reaction. We also say that antlers have a "memory" when there is absolutely no thought or mental process involved. The antler's memory is more a response to tropism, a response to an outside influence. Deer often produce non-typical antlers, year after year, in response to damage done earlier to the antler itself or to the pedicel.

Merriam elk (*C. e. merriami*)

This subspecies of elk was larger in body size than either the Rocky Mountain or Roosevelt elk. This is most unusual because its range was farther south than either of the other two subspecies. It was found in southern Arizona, New Mexico, western Texas, and Mexico. We really don't know how large a population there was of the Merriam elk. We do know that all of them had been killed by 1906.

Metabolism

The chemical conversion of food to provide energy and growth in a creature's body. Activity increases demand for caloric expenditure by the creature in order to supply the energy needed. The calories come from ingested food, accumulated fat, or the actual muscle tissue of the creature itself. The metabolism of small birds increases greatly in cold weather. The metabolism of all ruminants usually slows down drastically around December 1 and increases to normal around March 1. This is a tremendous survival factor for the ruminants at a time when food is scarce.

Metatarsal gland

The gland found on the outside of the deer's foot, halfway between its ankle and its hoof, is a gland that I believe is atrophying. It is characterized by having a cornified ridge surrounded by hair tufts. I have never been able to detect any

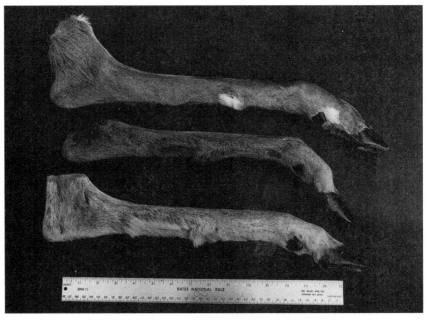

Top to bottom, the metatarsal glands of white-tailed, black-tailed, and mule deer.

odor coming from the gland, nor have I been able to detect a discharge of any kind. The size of the gland does provide concrete evidence of the species of deer from which it came. Whitetails have a one-inch gland, blacktails have a three-inch crescent-shaped gland, and mule deer have a five-inch slash. Interbreeding between the species produces a gland of variable size.

Micro-climate

A micro-climate is caused by the protection of an area from elements that create the ambient temperature. For example, white-tailed deer will seek out deer yards in the winter that are in low-lying, dense cover, usually composed of evergreens. The evergreens hold the snow aloft so it is easier for the deer to move about. The evergreens also stop the force of the wind, allowing the temperature to be higher in the yard than in the outside exposed areas. Mule deer like to lie up against south-facing large stones or cliffsides because the stones heat up ever so slightly on even the coldest days and reflect the sun in the daytime and give off some heat at night. The stones also deflect the wind.

Microorganisms

Small living organisms, such as bacteria, fungi, algae, and viruses that are so small that they must be viewed through a microscope. In a ruminant's paunch or rumen are many different types of microorganisms and microflora that help in the breakdown of the vegetative material that is eaten. In turn, many of them give off fatty acids that can go directly into the animal's bloodstream. These organisms also pass into the deer's abomasum, where they are digested along with the eaten food.

Migration

Caribou are among the most traveled of land mammals. While most of the herds migrate north and south, from the edge of

Caribou migration trail through tundra.

the boreal forest to the tundra region each spring and back again in the fall, some travel east and west. All of them usually travel hundreds of miles—and in some cases, a thousand miles or more—in migration. Elk, moose, and mule deer usually travel from the high elevations of their summer ranges to a winter lowland. These migrations may be as much as a hundred miles or more. With moose it is considerably less. Northern whitetails may migrate up to 50 to 75 miles, usually about 25 miles, from their summer range to a traditional yard for the winter. Southern whitetails may shift their home range in response to drought and lack of water; they don't move because of the cold.

Mock scrapes

I'm not sure if my good friend Bob McGuire was the first to make a mock scrape, but he was the first to publicize that it could be done. Bob reasoned that if you had a good spot to hunt from but there were no scrapes at that spot, you could attract the big bucks to stop there by making a mock scrape. He found that by cutting off the overhead branch of an active scrape and tying it where you wanted it, bucks could be induced to stop and scrape there. In addition to the overhead branch, he would scrape a depression beneath the branch and saturate the scrape with buck urine. Care must be taken not to get human scent on the overhead branch or in the scraped area. Mock scrapes do work. See *Primary scrapes.*

Molars

The last three teeth on both the top and bottom jawbone of humans, ruminants, and most animals. They are the last teeth to erupt through the jawbone and are not replaceable. Members of the canine and feline families don't have them as they don't chew their food.

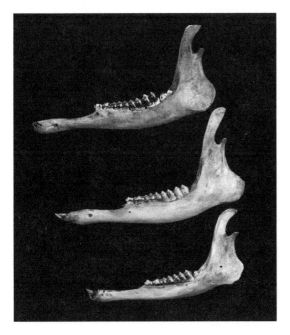

Jawbones of deer aged six months with one molar erupted, nine months with two molars erupted and one year with third molar erupting. (Bottom to top)

Molt

The annual shedding of hair that most animals do each spring as the long hair that kept them warm through the winter sloughs off. Elk, caribou, and moose shed their hair just once a year. Deer shed their hair twice a year, having both winter and summer coats.

Monarch

Occasionally, a bull elk will have eight or more points, or tines, on each main beam and will be referred to as a "monarch."

Monochrome

Most mammals, except primates, do not have the ability to see a full spectrum of color because they have no need to. Except for the bright face of a mandrill and the brightly colored rear end and scrotum of some of the primates, none of the mammals have bright colors. Most mammals have a single-based color (are monochromatic). Birds, fish, and insects are brightly colored and can see bright colors.

Monocular

Whereas you use both eyes with binoculars, you use just one eye with a monocular because it has only a single eyepiece. The advantage of using a monocular is that they are usually only one-third the size and weight of binoculars and can fit nicely into a jacket pocket. They can be purchased in all sizes and magnifications.

Monogamous

Monogamy means having just one mate. None of the Cervidae are monogamous. The biggest, best males do the bulk of the breeding.

Montane

Montane refers to mountainous country. Animals such as elk are said to be a montane species.

Moon phases

A moon that is growing larger is said to be waxing; a moon that is reducing in size after being full is waning. We have the new moon, half moon, full moon, half moon, and full again. Much research is being done to show that a deer's rutting activity is governed by the phase of the moon. My own research shows that the rutting season is still governed by photoperiodism.

Moose

The word moose comes from the Algonquin Indian word meaning "twig-eater," because of the moose's habit of browsing.

A bull moose browsing on twigs.

Moose sickness

Moose sickness is a common term for moose that have contacted the meningitis brainworm *Parelaphostrongylus* from the white-tailed deer. Infected moose usually walk in circles, stagger, and eventually are not able to stand or feed. It is only because moose are building up an immunity to this parasite that the herds in New England are expanding in population and range.

Mortality

It has been calculated that about 40 percent of all white-tailed fawns die or are killed during their first month of life. Predation on moose calves in some areas by grizzly bears takes as high as 80 percent. When any of the cervids lose up to one-third of their normal body weight through an exhausting rutting season or through starvation, they die.

Moss on a tree

Moss may grow on the north side of an isolated tree because moisture lasts longer there. Trees in a forest may have moss growing on all sides because the sun doesn't shine directly on the trunk. Using moss to tell direction is an unreliable method.

Mountain caribou

See *Woodland caribou.*

Mutant

Any deer that has a white coat and any spot of brown on it as large as a dime and does not have pink eyes is a mutant and not an albino. Mutants are the result of a genetic characteristic in which recessive genes are passed on from one generation to the next. Mutants often have lordosis and defective

A young mutant white-tailed buck.

hearing. (See *Lordosis.*) They are often shunned by the other deer because they are so conspicuous.

Mutual grooming

Mutual grooming is common among all members of the deer family, as the females lick their young to clean them at birth and to imprint them. It is most common among white-tailed adults, where both bucks and does commonly groom the other members of their fraternal or maternal group, forging strong bonds of family and friendship. Bucks, especially during the rutting season, lick each other's forehead scent glands.

Muzzleloader

Any gun where the powder and the ball are rammed down the barrel through the muzzle. Authentic muzzleloaders are fired by a spark ignited by a striking flint, a flintlock, or a fulminate of mercury cap, a caplock. Modern muzzleloaders strike the cap in the breech. Many states now have a special muzzleloading hunting season.

Leonard Lee Rue III with whitetail taken with a muzzleloading rifle.
Credit: Irene Vandermolen

Nasal gland

These are glands found just inside the nasal passageway of a deer. There is very little known about the function or importance of these particular glands.

Natal

Natal is the actual time of the birthing of any creature.

National Rifle Association (NRA)

The National Rifle Association is an organization that is in the forefront of protecting sportsmen's rights to own and use firearms of all kinds. They offer instruction in the use and safety of all types of firearms. They sponsor national shooting competitions. Every sportsman should belong to the NRA. Contact them by phone at 202-828-6240 or write NRA, 1600 Rhode Island Avenue NW, Washington, DC 20036.

Natural fluctuations

Nothing in nature follows a natural program; everything swings like a pendulum, moving between highs and lows. Weather, with its extremes of cold or heat or floods or droughts, affects food crops, survival rates, the stability of wildlife populations, and their well-being. The conditions affect the natural fluctuations in the numbers of the wildlife we see.

Natural mineral licks

All mammals need certain minerals in order to maintain health. Calcium is needed for strong bones in animals as well as in man. Plants growing on limestone soils are an excellent source of calcium. Unfortunately, many of the needed minerals have been lost through overexploitation of our soils by poor farming practices. Deer will instinctively feed on farm crops that have been fertilized.

There are many areas of this country where salt, sulphur, copper, lime, and other minerals will be brought to the sur-

Deer Hunter's Gallery

White-tailed buck, sniffing the air for danger. Credit: Leonard Lee Rue III

A rutting buck flehmening. Credit: Len Rue Jr.

Taking a midday snooze. Credit: Leonard Lee Rue III

Social grooming during a snowstorm. Credit: Leonard Lee Rue III

Two bucks sparring. Credit: Len Rue Jr.

A mutant deer (with normally colored eyes). Credit: Len Rue Jr.

A true albino, with pink eyes.
Credit: Leonard Lee Rue III

Two bucks take aggressive postures before fighting. Credit: Leonard Lee Rue III

Buck with antlers broken during a fight.
Credit: Leonard Lee Rue III

Huge bull moose feeds on underwater plants. Credit: Len Rue Jr.

A 6 x 6 trophy bull elk. Credit: Len Rue Jr.

Superb 5 x 5 mule deer buck, in the rut. Credit: Len Rue Jr.

A barren ground caribou bull in velvet.
Credit: Len Rue Jr.

Trophy white-tailed buck. Credit: Leonard Lee Rue III

face by spring water. Such natural mineral licks are known to all of the animals in the area, and each generation teaches the next generation where those springs are located. There is a natural "lick" on the farm next to where I live where the deer have eaten the soil, creating large holes. In the early days, pioneers visited such natural springs and boiled off the water to get salt. The "blue licks" in Kentucky were famous.

Necropsy

Wildlife biologists often perform a necropsy, an autopsy, on wildlife that is found dead in order to ascertain what caused the creature's death. When an emaciated carcass is found, it may be attributed to old age, but when a creature in apparently good condition is found, then disease is suspected. To protect the rest of the creatures the biologist must find out the cause of death.

Negative energy balance

In many deer wintering yards that have been used for generations, most of the good, nutritious browse tips have long since been eaten. The deer are forced to eat the older, larger-diameter browse, which has less nutrition than the tender twigs. It often costs the deer more in caloric expenditure to eat the coarser frozen twigs than it gets back in nutrition from the twigs it is eating. This causes a negative energy balance. The deer would do better not to eat at all.

Nematodes

Nematode is another name for the parasitic roundworms that, in many different forms, affect all of the Cervidae. The abdominal worms sometimes seen on the outside of a deer's intestines or liver are nematodes, as are the lungworms.

Neonates

The newborn of any creature is called a neonate by biologists.

Neoteny

The retention of juvenile characteristics when the creature has become an adult is known as neoteny. A good example is the fact that some adult deer retain vestiges of the spotted coats they had as fawns.

Niche

Technically, a niche is a crevice or a small hole in a wall to hold a statue. Biologically, a niche refers to every nook and cranny in the out-of-doors where some creature has adapted to be able to live there.

NIMBY

An acronym standing for Not In My Backyard. Many city dwellers are the most ardent preservationists and want to expand the range of all wild creatures, but they never come in contact with the creatures whose range they want to expand. They want to save everything; they want to expand the range of everything, but not in *their* backyard.

Nocturnal

A creature that carries on the bulk of its activities under the cover of darkness is said to be nocturnal. I believe that trophy white-tailed bucks, even during the rut, become strictly nocturnal.

Non-typical antlers

Most non-typical antlers are caused by accidents to the growing antlers or to the pedicels. Antlers that are damaged by accident one year often retain a "memory" and produce antlers that are non-typical every year thereafter, but to a lesser extent each year. Antlers that are non-typical because of damage to the pedicels, however, will usually be non-typical for the rest of the deer's life. Antlers that are non-typical due to the contralateral effect of injury to the foot or leg tend to outgrow the deformity unless the damage to the leg or foot is

White-tailed buck with two main beams on left antler.

permanent. Occasionally non-typical antlers are a genetic characteristic, and we don't really know why.

Northern woodland white-tailed deer (*O. v. borealis*)

This is one of the largest-bodied of the various subspecies of the white-tailed deer. The deer north of the Ohio River, west to Minnesota, in the southern portions of eastern Canada, and in all of New England south to Virginia belong to this

A northern woodland white-tailed buck.

subspecies. The Jordan buck, long the number one B&C head in America was a *borealis.*

Northwest white-tailed deer (*O. v. ochrourvs*)

This is also a very large-bodied, large-antlered subspecies. It is found in western Montana, Wyoming, Idaho, Washington, Oregon, northern California, and Nevada, and in southern British Columbia in Canada.

Northwestern moose (*A. a. andersoni*)

This subspecies of moose is found from Quebec west to the Yukon Territory and from the U.S. border north to the Arctic. It is larger than the eastern woodland moose, but not as large as the Alaskan-Yukon subspecies.

A northwestern white-tailed buck, from western Montana.

Nose bots

Nose or nasal bots are the larvae or worm forms of the common bot flies. The female flies lay their eggs around the noses of the Cervidae, which ingest the eggs when they lick their noses. The eggs hatch, and the larvae travel to the nasal region of the animals where they start to develop and are sneezed out. The pupae burrow into the ground, where they finish their development and emerge as adult flies.

Nursery band

This is most commonly seen in bands of elk, where groups of elk calves will band or group together and be watched over by unrelated females or "aunties" while their mothers are off feeding.

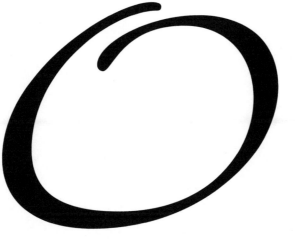

Olfactory

Anything that has to do with the sense of smell is olfactory.

Olfactory advertisement

Any of the chemical signals or communications sent out by one animal to another is, in essence, an olfactory advertisement. A dog urinating on a fire hydrant, a buck rubbing forehead scent on a sapling, and a doe dribbling pre-estrus urine are all forms of olfactory advertisement.

A white-tailed buck rubbing forehead scent on a tree.

Olfactory bulb

In the roof of the nasal passage are little hair-like cilia, or nerve endings, that trap incoming molecular odors and send them to the olfactory bulb, which transmits them directly to the brain as chemical impulses. There they are decoded into individual odors.

Omasum

The omasum is the third in line of the four compartments that make up a ruminant's stomach. It is characterized by having forty vertical flaps that alternate in height from ⅛ to 1⅛ inches. Both digestion and absorption take place here.

Opportunistic feeder

Although deer are properly known as specialized, or selective, feeders, they are also rightly known to be opportunistic feeders, as they often eat food that they don't usually eat. For example, deer love the twigs of ornamental yew trees, which are very expensive when purchased at nurseries. It's not the type of browse they would customarily eat, but eat it they do at every opportunity. It ordinarily takes the tips of four $80 yew trees to feed a deer for one day.

Orphaned

Because the young of all of the Cervidae live in a maternal society, the young are essentially orphaned if their mother dies or is killed. It should never be assumed that a fawn or an elk or moose calf is orphaned if you do not see the mother, because the young of these species are "hiders." The young depend upon remaining hidden to escape detection. The young of caribou are "followers" and usually escape predators by outrunning them if possible.

Osborne caribou

See *Woodland caribou.*

Outfitter

Many states require that non-residents hire a guide in order to hunt. The guide is also usually an outfitter that provides the horses, tents, bedrolls, cooking gear, food, and other gear, "the outfit" that you will need on your trip. There are good outfitters and not-so-good outfitters, as with every profession. Always contact any prospective outfitter and ask for the names and addresses of previous clients, and then contact those people to see if they were satisfied. Not every guide can produce a trophy animal every time, because that's not possible. Every outfitter can, and should, provide decent accommodations.

Ovary

The ovary is the part of a female's reproductive tract that produces the egg. It is the counterpart of the male's testes.

Overbrowsing

When a population of any member of the Cervidae becomes too large, they destroy their habitat by eating the vegetation faster than the plants and trees can produce it. Each type of plant has its own threshold for browsing. Some are very tolerant, while others die quickly. In time, the entire vegetation of an area can be changed by the elimination of favored species and the increase of more tolerant, sometimes undesirable, species.

Overhead branch

In almost every instance, a primary scrape will be made under an overhead branch. The buck usually chews on the branch

A white-tailed buck depositing saliva scent on a twig over a scrape. Credit: Len Rue, Jr.

first, depositing his saliva on it. He then rubs the branch over his preorbital, his forehead, and perhaps his nasal glands.

Overstory

A forest that reaches its climactic stage usually forms a solid canopy, or overstory, of branches that prevents sunlight from reaching the forest floor. The vegetation thus shaded dies, opening up the forest floor. This lack of diversity of vegetation caused by the overstory causes most climactic forests to have very little wildlife.

The overstory has killed all of the underbrush in this forest. The deer have been pawing through the snow for acorns, the only food available.

Ovulation

During the peak of the female's estrus period, a ripened ova, or egg, is discharged from her ovary into the fallopian tube and thence to her uterus, where it waits to be fertilized by a sperm from the male. The odor of the male and his courtship rituals help to stimulate the female to ovulate.

P

Pack horse

If you are going back into the mountains to hunt elk or mule deer, you undoubtedly will go by horse. Almost all western outfitters use them. Not meaning to offend any horse lovers, I have to state that most horses are the dumbest animals you will ever work with. Use a mule whenever possible, as they are more sure-footed and dependable. I was raised on a farm and worked with horses every day. I have been bitten, kicked, stomped on, thrown, and wiped off, and have had them try to roll with me on them—and that has happened, or will happen, to everyone working with horses. Do not leave your rifle in its scabbard when you get off the horse. Do not leave camera gear tied to the cantle of your saddle when you get off. If it can be broken, a horse will break it, and don't say I didn't warn you.

Palatable

Something that is edible is palatable. It may not be the most desirable food, or the most nutritious, but it can be eaten.

Palmated

The antlers of an adult bull moose are typically palmated, flattened like the palms of your hand, with points or tines projecting from the forward edge like your fingers. The "shovels" or brow tines of caribou are also palmated. The bez, or second, tine is usually palmated as is the main beam between the top points. Occasionally white-tailed bucks will have a palmation of the main beams. A friend of mine shot a Texas buck whose main beam looked like a miniature moose rack.

Panniers

If you go back in the mountains with most western outfitters, all of your camping and hunting gear will usually be carried on a pack horse. A wooden pack saddle will be strapped on

The palmated antlers of a huge Alaskan bull moose. Credit: Tim Lewis Rue

the horse and big wooden boxes, known as panniers, will be tied to the pack saddle. Make sure anything you carry into the mountains that you do not carry in your hand goes into the panniers for protection.

Panting

Panting is done by all members of the Cervidae. Panting is usually done in an effort to cool the body by cooling the blood as it passes through the lungs by the rapid exchange of internal heat with the outside air. Exertion while the weather is still warm and the animals have their winter coats will cause them to pant. Deer that are frightened or stressed pant heavily.

Papillae

Inside a cervid's paunch, or rumen, are little fingers of flesh about ¾ to 1 inch in length. There are about 1,000 of these papillae to the square inch. It is nature's way of greatly increasing the surface area of the paunch without actually making the paunch itself larger. The papillae help in breaking down the fibrous vegetation that has been eaten.

Papillomas

Deer often get large, wart-like growths on their outside skin that go by the name of cutaneous fibroma papillomas. These fibromas are caused by a virus that is spread among deer by biting flies and midges. Some of the fibromas become quite large, but unless they impair a deer's sight, they cause little harm. Cold weather kills the flies and midges and freezing weather usually causes the fibromas to freeze and fall off. The meat of a deer with fibromas is perfectly good to eat.

Parasites

An organism that lives on or in another creature from which it gets its nourishment at the expense of its host. These in-

The flies biting this deer for blood are parasites.

clude things from internal worms and nematodes to flies, ticks, and mosquitoes.

Parturition

The actual process of giving birth to young is known as parturition.

Pathogens

The viruses or bacteria that cause diseases are pathogens.

Patterning

The most successful hunters are the ones who do the most scouting, the ones who know where the deer are, what they are feeding upon, and where they are bedding. Deer are habitual creatures, and unless something disrupts them, they follow the same general pattern day after day. By patterning the bucks in your area, or even a particular buck, you greatly increase your chances of hunting success.

Paunch

The first and largest of the four segments of a cervid's stomach is its rumen or paunch. The food eaten initially goes into the paunch, which can hold eight to nine quarts and has the combined functions of storing the unchewed food and acting as a fermentation vat. After a deer has filled its paunch, it retires to some spot of comparative safety to chew its cud.

Peary's caribou (*R. t. pearyi*)

This is the smallest of the five subspecies of caribou. It has the northernmost range, being found only on Canada's Arctic Islands. Estimations put its entire population at between 10,000 and 15,000 animals. In keeping with the snow-covered regions, the Peary's caribou has a white coat.

Pedicel

The long protrusions that grow on the frontal skull plate of the Cervidae that form the base from which the antlers will grow. The pedicel forms on the skull where a special layer of tissue called the periosteum has been laid down.

The broken pedicel on this white-tailed buck caused its right antler to grow downward. Credit: Irene Vandermolen

Pedicel transplants

Experiments were done by Drs. Goss and Hartwig wherein they surgically removed the periosteum tissue from a deer's skull plates and replanted it on different parts of the deer's body. Fundamental antlers grew wherever the periosteum was implanted.

Pelage

Pelage is the proper term for hair that is over five one thousandths of an inch in diameter. Fur is usually less than five one thousandths of an inch. All of the Cervidae have mainly pelage as their primary coat of hair, although in the winter they also have very fine woolly underhair. The winter coats of the Cervidae have hollow hairs, filled with dead air, that provide excellent insulation. In the winter, the white-tailed deer has about 2,600 hairs to the square inch. In the summer, the white-tailed deer has about 5,200 hairs to the square inch, but the hairs are solid then, and short. Caribou, living farther north than the other Cervidae, have the warmest coats of hair of all.

Pelage color

The whitetail alone among the Cervidae undergoes the greatest change in pelage color. Its summer coat is a bright russet-red while its winter coat is a dark brownish-gray, according to the subspecies and its range.

Pellet count

In the spring, summer, and fall, deer usually defecate on the average of 36 times in a 24-hour period. In December through March, because of lowered metabolism and a shortage of food, the average is 12 times in a 24-hour period. Knowing this, biologists can go out in the winter over fresh snow and count the number of pellets in a given area and divide by 12 and have a fair idea of how many deer there are in that area. In the summer, the area has to be gone over twice because all of the pellet groups seen on the first trip have to be marked, usually sprayed with a vegetable dye. Then, on the second trip, all unsprayed pellet groups are counted. This is a very labor intensive method and seldom used.

Perlation

The bony, pointed projections and ridges that grow on the outside at the base of a deer's main antler beams. The amount

Heavy perlation on a whitetail's antler base.

of perlation on the beam grows with age. It is with the perlation that the buck actually grates the bark loose from the saplings that it rubs.

Peruke antlers

Members of the deer family that have been castrated, either intentionally or accidentally, do not grow normal sets of antlers. They often grow an accumulated mass of antlers, over the years, that have the tapered appearance of a beehive. These are known as peruke antlers.

Petroglyphs

Carvings or paintings done on cliff faces by Indian hunters thousands of years ago. Their depictions of deer, elk, and wild sheep may have been an account of their success as hunters, or they may have been imploring the "Great Spirit" to let them be successful in their upcoming hunt. At any rate, it proves the importance of these animals in their daily lives.

Pheromones

In its original usage, pheromones was the name given to the chemical odors given off by female moths and butterflies that sexually attracted the males to them. Today, it is the term generally given to any chemical sexual stimulant. For example, we know through biological experiments that urine, taken directly from a doe's bladder, does not stimulate the bucks as does urine that is discharged through the doe's urethra and comes into contact with her vaginal discharges. The pheromones are in the vaginal discharges.

Philopatry

The tendency of most birds and animals to stay in, or return to, their home area. More than a love of home, it is the intimate knowledge of their home areas that provides the creatures with their best chance of survival. For example, they know where to go to escape danger and find food, water, and shelter. It's why deer usually run in large circles.

Photoperiodism

Photoperiodism, the amount of daylight in a 24-hour period, is one of the greatest forces governing the activities of most living things in the world. It is the force that determines, with an exactness, when birds and animals migrate, breed, give birth, go into hibernation, emerge from hibernation in the spring, and so forth. In mammals, the amount of daylight is picked up through the eyes, via the optic nerve, which sends electrical impulses to the pineal gland. This gland, in turn, sends chemical signals to the pituitary gland, which causes the endocrine system to send hormones through the body, via the bloodstream, that either speed up or slow down the functions of the body. We humans, because of artificial lighting, are often out of sync with the environment, yet we, too, still basically respond to photoperiodism.

Pineal gland

The pineal gland is a small, pinecone-shaped gland located at the base of the brain. It is often referred to as "the third eye" because it receives information, directly from the eyes, about the amount of light available in a 24-hour period. The pineal gland secretes a hormone known as melatonin. When light begins to fade in the evening, the production of melatonin starts. In the morning, the production of melatonin stops. In winter, when the nights are long, the production of melatonin is high; in the summer, it is low. It is melatonin that signals the pituitary gland to increase or decrease the activity of the endocrine system.

Pioneer species

A pioneer species is a species that first moves in to take advantage of a habitat change. In the northern states, after an area has been clear-cut or burned over, berry bushes and annuals are the first plants to move in. The first pioneer trees are usually aspen, birch, or red cedar. This is also known as plant succession. Mice are the first mammals to take advantage of a regrowth area, followed by rabbits and hares. Deer move in as soon as there is browse enough to sustain them.

Plant succession

See *Pioneer species.*

Plantigrade

Animals that walk upon the entire foot surface are known as plantigrade animals. They include such creatures as

Bears, like humans, walk upon the entire foot and are known as plantigrade animals.

bears, raccoons, most members of the rodent family, and humans.

Play

All play is a conditioning for later life, whether in humans or animals. It increases lung capacity, heart muscles, speed, endurance, and strength. Deer fawns and elk calves play frequently. They play the same games our kids play: tag and

A young white-tailed buck is playing and jumping with exuberance.

running races. Deer also play hide-and-seek. I have not seen caribou and moose buck, jump, and run the way deer and elk do.

Poaching

Poaching is the illegal taking of wildlife, whether it is out of season, the wrong sex, the wrong method, or the wrong amount. It is conceded that, in many areas, the illegal taking of game animals may actually exceed the legal harvest. Poaching is wrong and must be stopped. Every game animal taken illegally is one that cannot be taken legally. The obsession that many hunters have today for trophy animals and the prices being paid for large sets of antlers and horns all conspire to promote poaching. As long as someone is willing to pay grossly inflated prices for a set of antlers so that he can get his name in the record book (also illegal), there will always be someone willing to poach the trophy animal. And that is a trophy that is no longer available to the legal hunter.

Poaching hotline

Most states now have a direct phone line that will reach a conservation officer at once if someone has a tip about a poaching incident. Some states even offer a reward on all tips that lead to a conviction. All states protect the identity of the person calling in the tip so they need have no fear of retribution from the poacher. The success of this program depends entirely upon you and me doing our duty by reporting poaching incidents so that the officers can do their job of protecting the wildlife and our hunting heritage.

Polychoke

Many shotgun hunters, having only one gun to use for hunting, install either a polychoke or choke tubes on the end of the barrel. The shotgun's barrel is usually cut off behind the choke boring and either of the two devices is installed. The polychoke, as its name implies, allows the hunter to have the full gamut of chokes by just turning the variable choke gauge. The tubes require that a different tube be screwed onto the end of the barrel according to the hunter's needs. These devices work well and give the hunter a much more versatile firearm.

The tightest choke is often full, providing the greatest constriction of the shot that is fired. The chokes range from extra-full, full, improved modified, modified, improved cylinder, and cylinder. The cylinder boring has no constriction at all, allowing the shot to scatter widely. The gauges used in shotguns today are .410, 28, 20, 16, 12, and 10.

Leonard Lee Rue III's Winchester Model 12 pump shotgun has a polychoke on the barrel.

Polyestrus

If a female of the Cervidae is not bred in her first estrus period, or breeds and does not conceive, she will come back into estrus approximately 28 days later and continue these cycles until she is bred. From personal research, I have proof that a white-tailed doe can re-cycle at least seven times before being bred.

Polygamous

Having more than one mate at the same time. We usually say that the males of the Cervidae are polygamous because the dominant males will breed with more than one female. I personally have seen white-tailed does accept more than one male during a single estrus period; therefore they would also be polygamous.

A bull elk guarding his harem. Credit: Len Rue, Jr.

Pope & Young Club

The Pope & Young Club, founded in 1961, is the official register of big game killed with a bow. It is patterned on the Boone & Crockett Club, which records kills with either a gun or a bow, but only those that meet their higher minimum standards. The club was originally started in 1957 as a part of the National Field Archery Association and was named after Dr. Saxton Pope and his hunting companion, Arthur Young. These two men are, undeniably, the fathers of modern archery hunting. (See *Ishi*.)

Popliteal gland

A small jellybean-sized gland that is grayish in color and buried in the fat directly in front of the deer's haunch on its hind legs. If left on, this gland will impart a bad flavor to the meat when cooked.

Population irruptions

The term used to describe an animal or bird population that is exploding beyond control. This usually happens when a species is introduced to an area where it has no natural predators. Or it occurs when all of the prey species' natural predators have been eliminated, which is what happened to the mule deer population on the Kaibab Plateau. It's happening today in sections of New Jersey and other states where urbanization is preventing the hunting of white-tailed deer.

Postnatal development

The natural development of any creature in its infancy; what occurs after birth.

Predator

In the true meaning of the word, a predator is any creature that eats another creature, whether it be a spider eating a fly, a robin eating a worm, a wolf pulling down a deer, or a human biting into a hamburger. While it is true that the

The grizzly bear is a major predator of moose calves.

human eating the hamburger did not kill the steer, it is only because someone killed the steer for him. We humans are predators and have our eyes on the front of our heads, as do wolves, cougars, hawks, and eagles, so that we have the binocular vision needed for the accurate depth perception needed to take a prey species. See *Prey species.*

Predator avoidance

The older females in any of the Cervidae have a much greater rate of survival for their young than do the more inexperienced, younger mothers. The older white-tailed does have the best birthing territories and the greatest recruitment rate because they choose territories that are not likely to be frequented by predators. I have seen moose cows give birth to their calves high in the mountains to avoid the grizzly bears that killed every moose calf they could find in the lowland willows.

Predator control

No predator wipes out its prey species entirely, because as the prey species becomes scarce, the fecundity of the predator drops sharply. This drop in predation allows the prey species to rebuild its population. However, predators can reduce the number of a prey species so much that, in order for the prey species to recover, human intervention is needed. To help the prey species, predators are hunted or trapped in designated areas by predator control officers.

Predator strategy

Deer employ many anti-predator strategies in order to survive. It is well-known that, where possible, deer prefer to bed on top of ridges in the daytime because rising thermals will carry up to the deer the odor of any predator below them. Does with newborn fawns will bed the fawns separately at a distance from one another so that if a predator should discover one fawn, it is not likely to discover its twin.

Preferential foods

We all have preferences for certain foods that we would like to eat. Most of us can't afford filet mignon every night. Wildlife also have foods they prefer over all others, with the main problem being that with our exploding deer population, all of the deer's preferred foods have long since been eaten. What the deer are eating now is what's available.

Premolars

The twelve premolars that grow in front of the twelve permanent molars of the Cervidae are all replaceable teeth. The premolars erupt through the jawbone within a day after the young are born. They are all replaced with permanent teeth by the time the young are 1½ years old. The third of the replaceable premolars of the whitetail have three cusps, or pointed tops, prior to 1½ years of age. When that premolar is replaced, the permanent premolar has only two cusps.

Prenatal

Meaning before the young is born; the period in which the fetus develops.

Preorbital gland

This is the gland in front of the eye of all members of the deer family. It also is known as the tear duct or lacrimal gland. This gland gives off a scent that the animals often deposit, as in the whitetail rubbing a branch, or by exposure to air, as in the case of the elk that flares this gland into a large rosette while bugling.

The preorbital gland is right in front of the deer's eyes.

Preputial gland

A gland that has been found in the skin at the tip of the white-tailed buck's penis sheath. It is not understood just what purpose this gland serves.

Prescapular gland

A small, jellybean-sized gland that is grayish in color and buried in the fat directly in front of the deer's scapula, or shoulder blade. This gland must be removed before the meat is cooked.

Prescribed burning

The Indians of the eastern woodlands were the first game managers on this continent. They fully understood that the whitetail thrived on regenerating brush and browse. To open areas in the virgin forests, the Indians set fire to the woodlands. This is a prescribed burn in its simplest form. Today, game managers will burn segments periodically to keep them in the brush stage, a process that benefits many different types of wildlife, not just deer.

Preservation of habitat

The preservation of habitat takes many forms. It may be as simple as shooting more deer so they don't destroy the habitat by overeating. Or it may be as complex as limiting urban sprawl so that there is habitat left to save. It is a concrete fact that you can reduce a wildlife population by hunting, but you wipe it out forever when you cover its habitat with concrete.

Preserve

A preserve does just what its name implies. It preserves or protects all of the wildlife in the area by not allowing any hunting. Even many private hunting clubs still set aside some of their land as a preserve in which the wildlife is not disturbed. Preserves act as reservoirs in that the surplus wildlife will leave the protected areas as their numbers increase.

Prey species

A prey species—such as mice, rabbits, or deer—is one that is eaten consistently by predators. Most predators have eyes on the front of their heads and can see about 170 degrees of a circle. Prey species have their eyes on the sides of their heads and can see 310 degrees or more of a circle. This allows the prey to watch for danger in almost a complete circle.

Primary scrapes

Almost all primary scrapes will be made under an overhead branch. The buck first chews on the branch, depositing saliva on the crushed twig tips. He may then hook the branch with his antlers. Then he will rub his forehead, preorbital, and perhaps his nasal glands against the branch, depositing scent there. He will paw the earth vigorously two or three times with his right front foot, then two or three times with his left front foot. Keeping his front feet in the pawed area, he will

A white-tailed buck pawing a primary scrape.

bring his back feet into the pawed area also. Balancing on his front feet, he will urinate on his tarsal, or hock, glands as he rubs his hind legs together. The urine runs down his tarsals and his hind legs over the pawed area. Finished, he walks off.

Deer often just paw the ground slightly without going through the full ritual done at primary scrapes. These slight pawings are known as secondary scrapes.

Proliferate

To increase rapidly. White-tailed deer, having an annual recruitment rate of about 40 percent under good conditions, are said to be prolific.

Proteins

Foods containing protein are essential to the cervids, which need a diet of at least 16 percent protein to achieve maximum growth in both body and antler size. Proteins are also the building blocks of life, being composed of chains of amino acids, and are a part of every cell in a creature's body.

Public land

Land that is owned by either the federal, state, or local government that is open to access by the general public. Some public lands are open to hunting; some are not. Hunting is allowed on some sections of national wildlife refuges. No hunting is allowed in national parks. Pennsylvania has done an outstanding job of buying hundreds of thousands of acres with money from the sale of hunting licenses. Although the land was bought and paid for by hunters, it is open to the general public, who use the land 85 percent of the time.

Pump-action rifle

The pump-action rifle, like the lever-action, was a rifle favored in the early 1900s. It was primarily a gun used for hunting in heavy brush and forested lands. The sliding pump action was fast and each stroke ejected the spent casing, pumped the new cartridge into the chamber, and cocked the hammer. Some pump rifles had external, or visible, hammers, while most of them had internal hammers.

Pump-action shotguns

Pump-action shotguns are very popular and have a fast action. They have a single barrel, and I have fitted mine with a polychoke adjusted according to the game I'm hunting. After the shell in the chamber has been fired, the trombone motion ejects the spent hull, loading the fresh shell and cocking the hammer. Almost all of the pump guns made today have internal hammers.

Hunter using a pump-action shotgun for deer.

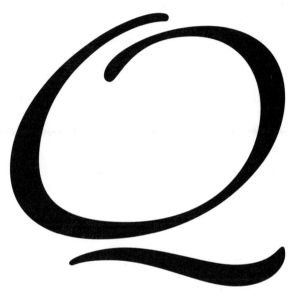

QDH or QDM

Those initials stand for one of the newest game management strategies: "quality deer hunting" or "quality deer management." It is a difficult policy to sell to the general hunting public because it means the deer herds must be reduced below the carrying capacity of the land. It means a larger percentage of does must be shot so that more food is available to the bucks, enabling them to grow larger antlers. It means that hunters will not be able to shoot every antlered animal they see. It means that hunters must pass up shots at spikes and four- and six-point bucks to give them time to grow old enough to grow trophy antlers. It means that many hunters may not get to shoot a buck at all for a number of years. It also means that, if the hunters are willing to make all of the sacrifices stated above, maybe—just maybe—for once in their life they will be able to shoot a truly trophy buck. Quality deer management is much more easily done in private preserves than on public land.

Quartering

In most states, the law requires that all the meat of big game animals must be packed out. Without having a horse or four-wheel vehicle to move the meat, a hunter must carry the meat out on his back. As it is not possible to move the entire carcass of such big animals as elk, moose, and even deer, the meat must be quartered to facilitate moving it.

To divide the carcass into four equal parts, it should be sawed or split down the backbone from the neck to the pelvic arch. Then a cut should be made, leaving the last three ribs on the hindquarter section. Such cuts are not practical, however.

The proper way to quarter an animal is to remove the loins on both sides of the backbone, so you don't mess up the meat when you saw through the backbone. Next, sever the backbone behind the ribs. Saw or chop through the backbone to the tail and through the pelvic arch to separate the hindquarters. Then split up the sternum, or the breastbone, and split or saw the backbone from the neck past the rib cage.

R

Rabies

Rabies is caused by a virus that is usually spread from one animal to another by biting. The virus passes to the bitten animal from the infected animal via the saliva. A very virulent disease, it usually kills the infected animal within a few days. People bitten by animals suspected of being rabid need to start a series of post-exposure vaccinations at once. There have been several cases of deer being infected with the rabies virus, but they do not transmit it.

Radiation

Normal body heat loss is usually due to radiation.

Radio collar

Our knowledge of all kinds of wildlife has been greatly expanded since the introduction of the radio collar. The wildlife is usually caught in nets, foot-snared, live-trapped, or darted. While under sedation, a small, sealed radio transmitter is attached to the animal's neck or back, or is inserted under the skin. Each transmitter emits its beeping signal on a different frequency so the biologists always know exactly which individual's collar is reporting. Using handheld receivers, or ones attached to a vehicle or airplane, the biologists are able to keep track of the creature's every movement. Transplanted wolves are fitted with a special collar so that if they leave a prescribed area the biologist can send a signal that causes the collar to inject the wolf with a sedative so it can be recaptured. With the use of radio collars, biologists have been able to ascertain animals' home ranges, daily movements, time of movements, and other insights into their daily lives.

Raghorn

A young bull elk, with the second set of antlers it grows when 2½ years old, is often referred to as a raghorn.

Raingear

You can't be comfortable if you are wet, whether from rain, snow, or perspiration. You should not wear tight-fitting outer rainwear if you are going to be active. I used to paddle a canoe a thousand miles each summer and wore rain pants and a poncho. The poncho kept me dry and allowed the free flow of air to prevent sweating. If you are going to be on a deer stand, you can wear one of the excellent waterproof garments that they make for duck hunting. I find Gore-tex to be too noisy for most purposes in deer hunting, especially if you pass brush. I still like to wear wool, which is warm even when wet, and I spray Scotchgard on it to make it water-repellent.

Rangefinder

A rangefinder is a device through which you look at your target and turn a knob until the two images are superimposed. A calibration on the dial will tell you exactly how far you are from your target. There is no point in sighting your gun for 100 yards if you are going to hunt in the heavily forested regions of the eastern United States. Conversely, if you are hunting in the open western states at ranges of 300 yards or more, then a rangefinder is invaluable. Many hunters sight in their rifles at 100, 200, or even 300 yards and then record where their particular bullet will raise or lower when shot at the different ranges. Distance can be hard to estimate; rangefingers correct that.

Rangifer

Rangifer was the Latin name given to the European reindeer by Baron Cuvier in 1827. As reindeer and caribou are conspecific, interbreeding readily, the species name is also used for the North American caribou.

Rattling

Rattling is done in imitation of a fight between two males. Although antler rattling is most often performed just for deer, slashing the brush with a stick is sometimes done while call-

Tom Fleming, the first person I personally knew to successfully call deer by rattling.

ing for elk and moose. Rattling antlers were used by the Indians thousands of years ago to entice deer into bow range. Today, in addition to using real deer antlers that have been cast or cut off, you can buy plastic antlers and rattling bags, bags with long pieces of hardwood. All of these sound good, but I prefer to use real antlers.

I firmly believe that medium-sized eight-point antlers are the best to use. The antlers of a really big buck are heavier and produce a lower tone when struck. The lower sound may scare the average buck out of the area because he is afraid to encounter a really big buck. I suggest that, at the start of each rattling session, the antlers only be "ticked" together lightly, as if the bucks were sparring. A loud crashing of antlers may scare off a buck that is hidden nearby. If, after a few minutes, no buck is seen, the antlers can be crashed together to get the sound out farther. Approximately 30 seconds of hard rattling and 10 minutes of watching is about the right timing. Remember, most buck fights only last five to 10 seconds.

Recoil

Recoil occurs in response to a basic law of physics wherein a force going in one direction produces an equal force going in the opposite direction. The amount of foot-pounds of pressure that pushes the projectiles out of any firearm barrel produces an equal amount of recoil back through the stock to the shooter's hand or shoulder. The heavier the gun, the less recoil is encountered, because it takes part of the recoil to overcome the inertia of the weight. The larger the gauge or caliber and the more powder in the shell or case to drive the larger projectile faster and farther, the greater the amount of recoil.

Recoil aids

A recoil pad may be as simple as a soft rubber pad to absorb part of the recoil. It may be an open-vented rubber pad that compresses to soften the recoil. Some of the more expensive guns will have a hydraulic piston built into the pad that works on the same principle as shock absorbers in automobiles. Some guns have slotted adapters as barrel extenders that capture some of the gases going out the barrel and direct them backward, lessening the recoil. Some guns have ported vents cut into the barrel that do the same job as the extenders do, but look neater.

Recreational value

No one can put a financial figure on the sheer enjoyment and pleasure that sixteen million Americans get from hunting the white-tailed deer alone. When you figure in the millions more that hunt mulies, blacktails, elk, caribou, and moose, the benefits are incalculable.

For many rural or wilderness communities all across North America, the money that hunters spend on licenses, hunting equipment, transportation, food, lodging, guides, and clothing is their main source of income throughout the year. It has been calculated that the money produced by hunting, if hunting were a company, would put it up among the top one hundred companies in the United States.

Recruitment rate

Basically, the recruitment rate is the number of young that were born and that survived to one year of age. Some game managers opt for a six-month period because, at six months, the fawns may be hunted in some states. Knowing the recruitment is very important because it is indicative of the health of the deer population and of the habitat. Where the habitat is poor because of a too-large deer population, the recruitment rate will be low because fewer fawns will be born and fewer of those born will live to be six months old. Under normal conditions on good range, the annual recruitment rate for white-tailed deer is 35 to 40 percent. It is much lower for elk, caribou, and moose, even on good range, because they usually produce singletons instead of twins.

Recurved bow

A recurved bow is similar to a traditional flat bow except that the ends of the bow have been steam-bent forward, which increases the speed of the bow by reflex action.

Regeneration

A term usually associated with the regrowth of a vegetative cycle that takes place after an area has been cleared by fire, disease, or clear-cutting. Seeds of many kinds are soon car-

Hunting deer with a recurve bow. Credit: Irene Vandermolen

ried in by the wind; seeds that may have lain dormant in the soil or seeds that may have had their cases opened by the fire soon begin to sprout. Nature abhors a vacuum, and no piece of land that is capable of producing vegetation lacks for vegetation for any length of time. Annual plants are the first to come in, then berry bushes, ferns, and perennials followed by seedlings from such pioneer trees as aspen, birch, sumac, and red cedar. As these grow, they provide the shade needed for the seedlings of hickory, ash, oak, pine, and others to grow. Eventually these latter trees will form a climax forest and they will shade out all of the other vegetation. A climax forest tends to stay a climax forest until it is killed by fire, disease, or clear-cutting.

Blackberries, a favored deer food, are some of the first plants to grow when a burned or cut-over forests regenerate.

Regulatory factors

There are both man-made and natural regulatory factors governing the populations of wildlife. The most important natural regulatory factors are water, food, and cover, in that order. No species can thrive where any one of these important factors is missing, even though some factors are more important than others. Man-made regulatory factors are the physical manipulation of the population of the species by hunting seasons, bag limits, and habitat management.

Regurgitation

All of the ruminants have a four-chambered stomach so that they can gather a lot of food quickly without having to take the time to chew it thoroughly. Under normal conditions, a whitetail can fill its paunch in about 40 minutes if good food is available. After filling their paunches, the ruminants retire to some place of safety where they can now take the time to masticate their food thoroughly. They regurgitate a cud, or bolus, from the stomach back up into their mouths, where it is thoroughly pulverized by the rotary chewing motion of their lower jaw. The cud is then re-swallowed, bypassing the paunch, or rumen, and going into the reticulum. Regurgitation is stopped whenever the deer becomes alert.

Rehabilitation

Every year, in late May or early June, all of the rehabilitation centers are flooded with white-tailed deer fawns that are picked up by well-meaning but misinformed people who think the fawns are orphaned. These folks don't know that it is the whitetail's survival tactic for the doe to stay away from

A three-day-old white-tailed fawn. Do not pick it up! Credit: Irene Vandermolen

her bedded fawns to prevent her body odor from attracting predators to the area. Unless you know that that particular fawn's doe is dead, unless you see her lying along the side of the road after being struck by a vehicle and you are sure the fawn you see belongs to the dead doe, the fawn you find is probably not an orphan.

Do not pick up or touch any fawns you find.

Not only is the fawn probably not an orphan, but it is also illegal in most states for you to pick up fawns. In almost every instance, the doe stands hidden, watching you "abduct" her fawn. Leave the fawn where you find it, get out of the area, and the doe will come back to the fawn when she deems it safe to do so.

Rehabilitation programs

Every state has people who have been licensed by the state to aid in the rehabilitation of orphaned, sick, or injured wildlife. There is a great deal of time, effort, and money involved in caring for these creatures, and basic veterinary knowledge is essential. The states are always looking for dedicated individuals to aid in this program. There is a National Wildlife Rehabilitation Association that provides complete and up-to-date information on the proper care of all creatures. They can be reached by telephoning 320-259-4096 or by writing to 14 N 7th Avenue, St. Cloud, MN 56303.

Reindeer (*Rangifer tarandus*)

The reindeer is the European counterpart of our North American caribou. It is a smaller, much more aggressive animal and most have been domesticated for thousands of years. The aggressiveness of the bulls is the result of domestication and their lack of fear of man. Thousands of reindeer were imported into Alaska in the past years to provide the Eskimos with a stable food supply. However, Eskimos are hunters, not herders, and the experiment failed. Reindeer and caribou readily interbreed, but this does not benefit the caribou as the offspring are smaller. There are several small herds in Alaska, with the one on St. Paul Island in the Pribilofs numbering about 800 animals.

Reload

Many hunters reload their own cartridges and shells. Great care must be taken in the measurement of the powder so as not to build up too much pressure. Anyone with the time and knowledge can save money by reloading their own shells as all the components are cheaper than buying factory loads. Over time, and with skill, rifle and pistol ammunition can be worked up that will produce greater accuracy than is possible with assembly-line ammunition.

Researchers

A researcher may be a scientific biologist or anyone deeply concerned with searching out new information about any

Leonard Lee Rue III, the author, photographing whitetailed deer. Credit: Len Rue Jr.

species. The white-tailed deer is probably the most studied, most thoroughly researched animal species in North America. I can personally vouch for the fact that, after 62 years of studying the whitetail, I continue to find new information all the time.

Responses to harassment

Different species have different tolerance levels to different types of harassment. It also has to do with the adaptability of the species. For example, whitetails often feed peacefully alongside army artillery ranges, paying no attention to the exploding shells. We have all seen whitetails totally oblivious to the traffic as they feed on a right-of-way. If whitetails are pushed by dogs, they will run in a circle but return to their favored bedding areas as soon as possible. Elk usually take off for heavily timbered areas of the high country when disturbed and may not come back. Moose retreat into the dense boreal forests and will stay away from areas where they have been disturbed several times. Caribou usually live in such remote areas that, except during the hunting season, they seldom encounter humans. As caribou are usually on the move all of the time, they just keep going when disturbed. Sometimes the caribou will make a mile-wide circle to come back to see what it was that disturbed them in the first place.

Restocking

Restocking of the Cervidae is done in an effort to bring back species to areas from which they were extirpated or to areas in which they were never found. There was a tremendous amount of restocking of whitetails from the late 1800s up to about 1930. The whitetails had been greatly reduced and their population was at an all-time low from 1890 to 1900. Today there is very little restocking of whitetails being done because almost every area that can support whitetails already has them. There is no shortage of whitetails. Moose are being successfully restocked in Colorado. A restocking of woodland

Elk are being restocked in states from which they have been extirpated for years.

caribou in Maine has failed. Elk have recently been reintroduced into Kentucky and plans are being made to restock them in Tennessee.

Reticulum

The reticulum is the second compartment in a deer's stomach. After food has been regurgitated from the rumen, thoroughly chewed, and re-swallowed, it goes to the reticulum. The reticulum has a lining that looks like a honeycomb, with hexagonal ridges about ⅜ inch apart. Each ridge is about ⅛ inch high. The reticulum can hold foodstuffs up to about the size of a standard baseball. Some digestion takes place in the reticulum, but one of its main functions is to filter out all foreign material. I have found stones, a .22-caliber cartridge case and even a piece of melted glass in deer reticulums that I have examined.

Rifle sticks

Almost all European big game hunters use a walking stick when hunting. When they shoot, they use this staff as additional support to help steady their rifles. Some of the hunters carry two loose sticks that they hold like a long shears, forming a bipod, which makes for even more steadiness in shooting. Rifle sticks are becoming more popular among hunters in the mountainous areas of North America.

Rifled slugs

Because all shotguns are smooth bores, having no rifling in their barrels, various companies put out mushroom-shaped slugs that have rifling, or grooves, molded into the slug to make them spin. The rifling on the slugs gives them greater accuracy than the round "pumpkin" or "Minnie" balls that were formerly used.

Rifles

Basically, a rifle is a firearm that has a series of slow twists and grooves cut into the inside of the barrel. The open "lands," the metal between the grooves, are the exact diameter of a projectile. The grooves cause the bullet to spin as it travels through the air, allowing for much greater accuracy and distance. There are many different actions that deliver the cartridge to the chamber.

Riparian

Riparian has to do with a riverbank. You often hear of how overgrazing by cattle has destroyed all the grass and brush in the riparian areas. Riverbank brush is critical as cover for whitetails.

Hunting deer with a bolt-action rifle. Credit: Irene Vandermolen

Roadkill

Pennsylvania has more deer killed on its highways annually, about 48,000, than some of the smaller states have harvested by hunters. As our human population explodes, coinciding with an explosion in the deer population, there are more cars on the road and more deer-related traffic accidents. With more than 500,000 accidents a year costing over one billion dollars in damage and resulting in over 200,000 injuries and 200 deaths, the game departments are being forced to reduce their deer populations.

Most states now allow people to pick up and utilize game animals that have been struck by motor vehicles. All states should allow, and encourage, this to prevent the loss of thousands of tons of good meat every year. I have picked up hundreds of freshly killed deer. Most states require that you notify the game department or the state police when you pick up road-killed animals so that you can take legal possession of them.

Roar

Whereas the North American elk's high-pitched call is known as "bugling," the European red deer, the elk's counterpart, is said to "roar." The sounds are quite similar, but the red deer's roar is much lower pitched.

Rocky Mountain elk (*C. e. nelsoni*)

This subspecies of elk is the most populous in number, has the greatest range, and is being transplanted to many parts of the continent. This elk is found in the Rocky Mountains from Alberta and British Columbia in Canada, south into Arizona and New Mexico. When people think elk, they think of this subspecies.

Rocky Mountain Elk Foundation

The Rocky Mountain Elk Foundation, headquartered in Missoula, Montana, is a national organization with members and chapters in all 50 states. The RMEF's main objective is the conservation of elk, and this is done by buying land needed for wintering ranges and migration corridors. The foundation runs feasibility studies and has been successful in re-establishing elk in much of their former range. Most recently the RMEF re-established elk in Kentucky, North Carolina, and Tennessee, and is currently trying to get them back into New York State's Adirondack Park. The RMEF provides disease-free animals for restocking. The major publication of the foundation is *The Bugle.* Their address is P.O. Box 8249, Missoula, MT 59807.

Rocky Mountain mule deer (*O. h. henionus*)

This subspecies is the prototype for mule deer. It is the largest and darkest of the eight subspecies. Its numbers have been steadily declining because of the habitat destruction by humans and competition by the invasion of the whitetail. However, it is expanding its range. I have personally seen them as far north as the Yukon border in Canada. It is found in all the Rocky Mountain states as far south as Arizona and New Mexico and has spread into the prairie states of the Dakotas and Nebraska. It is also found in Washington, Oregon, Nevada, and northeastern California.

A Rocky Mountain mule deer buck in velvet.

Rocky Mountain spotted fever

A disease spread to man by the arthropod *Dermacenter andersoni,* the Rocky Mountain wood tick. Whitetails are not a host, although mulies, blacktails, and elk are. The same precautions should be taken in handling these animals as you would take when handling whitetails to avoid the Lyme disease–carrying tick Ixodes. Again, I want to emphasize, spray your clothing with Permanone, a proven tick killer available from the Rue catalog: 800-734-2568.

Roosevelt elk (*C. e. roosevelti*)

This is the largest subspecies of elk in North America. Elk of this type that were taken to Admiralty Island, Alaska, have

A Roosevelt elk bull.

had recorded weights of over 1,100 pounds. It is a darker animal, as would be expected of one that lives in the coastal rainforests of British Columbia, Washington, Oregon, and northern California. Its antlers are heavier-beamed than those of the other elk subspecies, and they have a tendency to form a crown on the top.

Roosevelt, Theodore

Teddy Roosevelt (1858–1919), our 26th president, was an international big game hunter and an ardent conservationist. As president, he established many national parks, set aside refuges, and created governmental departments to care for the environment. He was one of the founders of the Boone & Crockett Club, the official register of all U.S. big-game trophies. The "teddy bear" that children love bore his name after he rescued a bear cub from a southwestern forest fire. America owes him a debt of gratitude for the land he preserved way back then for our use and pleasure today.

Royal bull

When the fifth, sixth, and seventh points, or tines, on the main antler beam of either the elk or the red deer form a basket, the animal is referred to as royal.

Rub lines

Rub lines are created by white-tailed bucks rubbing a series of saplings on the trail leading to and from their bedding area. I do not believe that the bucks are deliberately creating a line of rubs; I think it is just a coincidence that the rubs appear in a line because the buck just happens to make them as he walks the trail or patrols along the edge of a field.

Rub-urination

All whitetails, blacktails, and mule deer do rub-urination. They may do it at any time of the year, but they do it most fre-

A mule deer buck rub-urinating. Credit: Irene Vandermolen

quently during the rutting season. The more dominant the buck, the more frequently he urinates on his tarsal, or hock, glands and the darker they become. You can tell the dominant buck in a group simply by checking the color of the hair around his tarsal glands. Fawns start to rub-urinate when they are just one week old. Whereas strange dogs sniff each other's anal glands, strange deer sniff each other's tarsal glands.

In rub-urination, the deer balance on their front feet and hump their backs so that their urine trickles down over the long, clustered hairs on the tarsal glands of their hind legs. The deer then rub the tarsal gland of one leg against the other. Some of the urine is retained on the hairs by the lipids that are there, where bacterial action gives it a distinctive musky odor and dark color. The rest of the urine carries some of the lipids down the deer's foot, creating dark streaks down to the hooves.

Rubs

Rubs are made by all of the Cervidae, and they make them for different purposes. The first rubs are made to remove the velvet from their antlers. After that, the primary purpose of the rubbing is to strengthen the male's neck muscles in preparation for whatever fighting may take place later. The males put tremendous effort in their rubbing as they shred off the bark and gouge channels into the living wood beneath. You can easily see that the animals are using all their strength. I have seen both caribou and bull moose deliberately tangle their antlers into brush and pull the brush, roots and all, right out of the soil. I have seen whitetails push so hard that their back feet come off the ground.

All of the cervids also use the rubs as chemical scent stations and deposit mainly forehead gland scent, but also saliva, in the rubs. The rubs also are a visual means of com-

A white-tailed buck making a buck rub.

A bull elk making a rub.

munication because the white wood exposed by the rubbing can be seen for a long way.

Rubs are very attractive to females, and I have seen many white-tailed does investigate them by smelling them. I have also seen the does, on several occasions, lick the rubs and also rub their own forehead scent on the rubs.

Rue's Rule

Bergmann's Rule states that animals of the same species will be larger the farther north or south of the equator they are found. (See *Bergmann's Rule.*) Bergmann's Rule is basically true; however, it doesn't go far enough, so I wrote Rue's Rule to amend Bergmann's. Rue's Rule states, "The farther north or south of the equator they are found, the larger the members of the same species will be, so long as their preferred food is abundant and meets their nutritional needs; body size decreases in direct proportion to decreasing food supplies." The Peary's caribou is a good example of this rule, it being much smaller in size than either the woodland or barren ground subspecies.

Rumen

See *Paunch.*

Ruminants

All of the cud-chewing animals with four-chambered stomach are known as ruminants. This includes all of the cervids, wild and domestic goats, sheep, cattle, bison, and antelope.

Rut

The rut is the period of time when all of the male cervids are actively seeking out estrus females to breed. The rutting season is the time of the greatest activity of the year and the one time when the males are less cautious than usual. The peak of the rut varies with the different species because of the difference in their periods of gestation. The peak of the breeding season occurs so that the young of all species will be born at the most optimal time in the spring. The peak of the rut can vary within the species where the range is large, as in the whitetail. The peak of the breeding season for elk is around September 15, for caribou and moose the first part of October, for the northern deer November 10–17, and for the southern deer the last week of December and the first week in January. The white-tailed bucks are capable of breeding from the time they peel the velvet from their antlers, but September is primarily spent in building up the fat reserves on their bodies. No does are receptive at that time. The rut starts in mid-October, when increased levels

A buck is in the rut as long as his neck is swollen. Credit: Irene Vandermolen

of testosterone cause the bucks' necks to swell. The peak of the rut coincides with the peak of the does' estrus cycle from about November 10–17. For northern whitetails, the rut is over around December 15, when testosterone levels diminish and the swelling goes out of the bucks' necks. However, even though the rut is over and the bucks' antlers may be cast shortly thereafter, some of the white-tailed bucks are still capable of breeding as late as the first part of April.

S

Safety belt

Do not climb trees without a safety belt. Make sure the belt it-self is made of wide webbing or leather so that, if you do ever hang from it, it will not cut into your body as a narrow one would do. If you are climbing a tree that has no limbs for you to climb over, a single rope is sufficient to wrap around the tree. If you have to cross limbs, use two ropes so that you can fasten one rope above the limb before you unfasten the one below the limb and vice versa. When you climb, be sure to have one rope around the tree and fastened securely to your belt at all times.

Safety zones

In many states, such as New Jersey, because of our high human population and development, only shotguns or muzzleloading rifles may be used. No one is allowed to hunt within 450 feet of a house. That means, if the houses are 900 feet apart, there can be no hunting. This distance has been chosen because it is beyond the range of shotgun buckshot. Because of these safety zones, many deer never leave the protected areas. Thus, the bucks are becoming bigger because they are getting older. Such areas are producing trophy animals.

Salivary glands

A human's salivary glands are in the bottom of the mouth and produce about 1½ quarts of saliva a day. All of the cervids drip drops and drool long strips of saliva, but it comes from the top of the mouth. By my calculations, done with an eyedropper, a white-tailed buck drips between 1½ to 2 quarts of saliva a day. The more sexually active the buck, the more he drips or drools. Naturally, there is a difference in the amount of saliva drooled among the different bucks.

Salt blocks

Although all members of the Cervidae family can be lured to salt blocks, they are most often used to attract deer. When asked by hunters if they should put out salt blocks, I always suggest that they put out mineral blocks instead. With the latter, the deer get the minerals they need as well as salt. I personally use Deer Lix, which is a mineral concentrate that I then mix with granulated red mineral salts. The deer love it. Deer Lix can be purchased by calling Keith Stroud at 706-592-9004, or by writing him at 4894 Old Waynesboro Road, Augusta, GA 30815.

All hunters should put out minerals and salt for deer, but check your state's laws before hunting near such areas. Some states classify salt as bait and consider its use in the hunting season as illegal.

Scope

The word scope is a shortened version of the word telescope, which is basically what a scope is, a telescope with an internal reticle used for sighting. Scopes are now made for rifles, slug shotguns, handguns, and even for bows. They come in a vast array of sizes, powers, reticles, and costs. They are made in a fixed power of magnification or are variable, going from say 2X to 7X. The reticle inside, which is adjustable from the outside, comes in crosshairs, posts of all shapes and thicknesses, a combination of both, or a dot. The sight adjustment is usually done with a coin-slotted ¼-click micrometer adjustment. Each ¼-click will move the scope sight ¼ inch at 100 yards, taking four clicks to move it one inch. A common mistake is to use too powerful a scope, thinking it will allow you to see your target better, which it will only if the target is at a distance. For hunting in the eastern woodlands, a 1.5X to 4X scope is most commonly used. In the more open western areas, the 2X to 7X scopes are preferred. Remember, as in anything else, you get the quality you pay for. Buy the best scope you can afford.

Scope covers

Scopes should always be covered when not in use to protect the expensive optical glass of which they are made. Most scopes have removable fitted hoods that go over each end of the scope. Some scopes have hoods that are an integral part of the scope that flip up out of the way when the scope is being used.

Scope rings

Scopes must be fitted to the barrel of the gun, and this is usually done with a set of scope rings. Most of the rings fit into dovetailed notches, and the scope is left on the gun permanently. Others fit onto a bar that allows the scope to be removed from the rifle and snapped back in place when needed.

Scouting

The most successful hunters are the ones who have done the most scouting. A hunter must take the time to locate the areas where deer are most commonly seen and, if possible, to pattern the bucks. Knowledge of the deer's feeding and bedding areas, funnels, rub lines, primary scrapes, licking sticks, trails, and so forth is essential. The very best hunters scout all year long just because they so thoroughly enjoy seeing deer. They track deer in the snow, look for shed antlers in the spring, and search for bucks in velvet in the summer. They

By scouting for deer in the off-season, you will know where big bucks may be found in the next hunting season.

look for deer at every opportunity and it pays off. These are the hunters you see posing for pictures with the big bucks.

Screwworm

At one time the screwworm was the greatest killer of fawns in the southern states. Because infestations of these parasites also killed cattle, the United States government started an eradication project in 1958. The female screwworm laid her eggs on the umbilical cords of the newborn calves and fawns or in areas opened to infection by tick bites. The screwworm larvae ate the tissue at the site of infection, which either directly killed the fawns or allowed other infections to do so. While ranchers could treat the calves, up to 80 percent of most fawn crops were lost.

The government sterilized millions of male screwworm flies with cobalt treatments and released them to breed with females, which then laid infertile eggs. The huge herds of deer in our southern states were made possible only because of the success of that program.

Scrotum

The skin pouch containing the male's testicles or testes. The scrotum shrinks in size after the breeding season and draws up higher to the body for protection in cold weather. In August, due to photoperiodism, the testicles enlarge as they produce more of the male hormone testosterone, which causes the Cervidae bucks' and bulls' antlers to solidify. As the testicles enlarge, the scrotum drops farther from the body to keep the testicles cooler. The slight decrease in external temperature helps to ensure that the sperm in the testicles will be viable. It takes a very small increase in external temperature to render sperm infertile.

Sebaceous glands

Sebaceous glands produce sebum, the oily or fatty secretion that comes through the skin by a duct or alongside hair follicles. It is the sebum that waterproofs the coat of hair of all of the cervids. It is the lipids that trap the urine on the cervids' tarsal glands.

Second rut

For the white-tailed deer over most of North America, north of the 32nd parallel, the primary rutting season occurs November 10–17. Does that are not bred, or are bred and do not conceive, during that period re-cycle 28 days later and come in estrus during the so-called "second rut," which occurs December 8–15.

Doe fawns that have achieved a body weight of about 80 pounds may also breed during this period. Body weight is the critical factor in the fawns being mature enough to breed, and most of them need the extra month to attain it.

Secondary forest

There is almost no virgin forest left in the eastern United States. At some time almost every acre has either been cut off or burned over. At one time Vermont was 85 percent farm-

Female fawns that have achieved a body weight of 80 pounds by December may be bred in the second rut.

land and 15 percent forest. Today those figures have reversed themselves so that almost 85 percent of Vermont is now covered with secondary, or second growth, forests.

Segregate

To keep separate. The males of all of the cervids keep separate from the females except during the breeding season. Even caribou, which are in herds that travel constantly, usually travel in separate herds. With elk and mule deer, the males usually spend the summer higher in the mountains than do the females with young. In fall, when snow begins to force these animals to lower elevations, the females travel first with the males following. In the spring it is the female caribou, elk, and mule deer that start moving back to their summering areas first. Even though whitetails, over most of their range, do not migrate, they stay apart from one another even if on the same range. With the northern deer that do migrate to traditional yarding areas, it is the females who are on the move first.

Selective feeders

Deer are the most selective feeders of all of the cervids. Their narrow mouth allows them to more easily select a single type of vegetation from among many. The larger body size of the other cervids allows them to eat and digest far more coarse vegetation.

Selective harvest

Most states, according to their game management plans, require a selective harvest of the different cervids. Because the moose population has been low, in the few states that have moose, the law has allowed only bulls to be taken. The females are needed to build up the moose population. In my home state of New Jersey, you are required to shoot one doe before it is legal for you to shoot a buck. This is done in an effort to reduce the breeding potential of the deer herd so that the population can be controlled. That's selective harvesting.

Selenium

Deer that live on soils that have been depleted of selenium may have a higher than normal incidence of stillborn fawns. Although deer need just a trace of this mineral, they do require some.

Seral stage

Each successive stage in the sequence of plant types, from the first to the climax, is known as a seral stage. See *Plant succession.*

Seton, Ernest Thompson

Ernest Thompson Seton (1860–1946) was born in England, grew up in the Canadian prairie provinces, and later lived in the western United States. One of the greatest naturalists of all time, he was, and is, known for his extensive knowledge of all types of wildlife and for his thousands upon thousands of drawings and paintings. He was the author of dozens of books and co-founder of the Boy Scouts of America. His detailed anatomical depictions of wildlife were a force shaping my own photographic career and wildlife research.

Sexual maturity

Sexual maturity means being physically capable of breeding. All of the cervids, both male and female, are capable of breeding at 1½ years of age. However, being capable of breeding and being allowed to breed are two different things. While all of the females will be bred, the dominant males of each of the species will do everything in their power to prevent the young males from breeding. The constant chemical signposts of the dominant males cause the young bucks' brains to produce corticoids, which suppress their libido, thus helping to keep the turmoil of the rutting season to a minimum. It is believed that the extra quiescent year that the corticoids provide for the young males allows them to grow larger and stronger, making them better animals when they

Although this young white-tailed buck is sexually mature enough to breed, he will be prevented from doing so by the big bucks.

are ready to breed. In areas where most of the adult males are shot, particularly in whitetail societies, the young bucks create a chaotic condition with their excessive chasing. This chaos results in the entire herd entering winter in much poorer condition, reducing their chances of survival.

Ordinarily, the female matures at 2½ years of age, but, in deer, if the young female achieves a body weight of 70 to 80 pounds at the age of six to seven months, she may be mature enough to breed. In the rich farmland country of the Midwest, about 80 percent of all female white-tailed fawns breed at the age of six to seven months. In my home state of New Jersey, 40 to 60 percent of our female fawns are capable of breeding according to the part of the state they inhabit. In

Vermont, New Hampshire, Maine, and the rest of New England, almost none of the female fawns breed because they don't achieve the needed weight.

Occasionally, in areas of rich farm soil, some of the young seven-month-old white-tailed bucks develop little antlers that actually protrude through the skin and peel. These little bucks are capable of breeding, but they would not be allowed to do so by the adult bucks. They would not be capable of breeding an adult doe in any area because of their body size difference.

Shed antlers

Hunting sheds. That is what a lot of the hunters do each spring. Biologists claim that the antlers are cast, not shed, but it's the same thing; the antlers fall off. Hunting for antlers is not only a lot of fun, but it's the best way of knowing positively the size of the bucks that have made it through the sea-

White-tailed buck with one antler shed.

son and should be in the same general area to be hunted next year. Scouting for the next hunting season actually starts with hunting sheds.

Shiras moose (*A. a. shirasi*)

This smallest subspecies of the moose is restricted to the Rocky Mountain regions of British Columbia and Alberta in Canada and Montana, Idaho, and Wyoming in the United States. Transplants of this subspecies are being made into Colorado. A characteristic of this subspecies is that the main palms of many of the big bulls' antlers fold up and inward creating a basket effect.

A Shiras bull moose in Yellowstone National Park. Credit: Len Rue, Jr.

Shoe pacs

The boot that made L. L. Bean famous. Designed by Leon Bean many years ago, the boot has a rubber bottom and a leather top, an ideal combination to wear in flat areas where snow and slush are common. Many companies now make shoe pacs, and with the felt liners for extra warmth they are extremely popular footwear with hunters across the continent.

The only terrain where they put a hunter at a disadvantage is in the mountains, where they tend to slide on slopes. Lug-type soles are better in mountainous situations.

Shooting lane

Whenever possible, shooting lanes should be cleared in every direction from where you plan to stand. It doesn't matter if you are going to be up in a tree stand or using a ground blind. You must have cleared avenues through which to shoot if it is at all possible. The tiniest twig may be sufficient to deflect either an arrow or a bullet. I use shooting lanes for photography also because I don't want brush in front of my subject's eye. The little folding pocket saws or pruning shears are ideal for cutting twigs out of the way. Naturally, if you are driving deer, you won't have a chance to have shooting lanes, but the standers should take the time to clear the lanes if possible.

Shooting preserves

Shooting preserves have blossomed all over the country to provide hunting experiences for people who do not have the time, or do not want to take the time, to hunt under wilderness conditions. These preserves range in size from huge tracts of land of thousands of acres to areas that may be only 100 acres.

On the huge preserves, the animals are usually raised on the land and live under natural conditions, although they are fed supplemental rations to increase antler and body size. On the smaller preserves, the animals are purchased from farmers who raise them; they are released prior to the client's arrival to shoot them. The costs are usually much higher at the larger preserves. In either case, a trophy is often guaranteed, although no animal shot under these conditions can be entered in the Boone & Crockett trophy records, as it does not constitute "fair chase."

Shooting range

While it is comparatively easy to find a shooting range for handguns because they are indoors, it is becoming harder to find a rifle range. Contact your local sporting goods dealer or write to the National Rifle Association at 11250 Waples Mill Road, Fairfax, VA 22030; 703-267-1000; most ranges are listed with them. All guns must be sighted in before being used, and sighting is best done from a benchrest at a shooting range.

Most ammunition companies put out charts showing where each weight bullet crosses the line of sight twice when sighted at 100 yards. Do your initial sighting using the closest distance, which is approximately 25 feet. Most scopes move their internal crosshairs or posts so that one adjustment click moves the bullet impact point ¼ inch at 100 yards. Test firing should be done in groups of three, so that the shooter can be sure where the scope is sighted. Random shots are the shooter's fault. If your first group of shots is two inches high and one inch to the left, simply move your elevation eight clicks down and four clicks to the right and you should be close to being on target at 100 yards.

Shot placement

Every hunter tries to make a killing shot so that the animal drops in its tracks. No one wants to injure an animal. No one wants to have a wounded animal run off to die where it won't be found. That's why shot placement is important. Basically, any shot that goes into the rib cage should be a killing shot because the heart, lungs, and liver are all contained within the rib cage. A deer's heart is about two to three inches back from its elbow and two to three inches up from the bottom of its rib cage. An elk's or caribou's heart is four to five inches

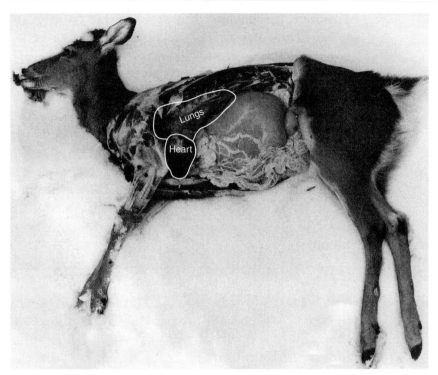

Knowing where the deer's vital organs are located is important for good shot placement. Shown are the heart and lungs.

back from the elbow and four to five inches up from the bottom of its rib cage. A moose's heart is about six inches back from its elbow and about six inches up from the bottom of its rib cage. Study the adjacent photo to aid you in where to place your shot. Remember, if you don't have a clear shot, if you are not sure that you can drop your quarry, *don't shoot.*

Shotguns

A shotgun is a smooth-bored firearm that has no rifling in the barrel. Most shotgun barrels are tapered at the distal end and narrowing them slightly produces various chokes.

Shovels

Most caribou bulls have a vertically flattened brow tine on their antlers known as a shovel. Usually only one antler has this palmated antler tine. When a caribou has one on each antler, the formation is called a double shovel. No, the caribou do not use their "shovels" to clear away the snow to find their food. To get to the moss and grass beneath the snow, the caribou paw away the snow with their hooves.

Shrub

A shrub is intermediate in size between a bush, which grows at most about six feet high, and a tree, which grows beyond 25 feet. A good example of a shrub is a dogwood or redbud because they seldom grow beyond 25 feet in height.

Siblings

Siblings are young born to the same father and mother. Twin white-tailed fawns are siblings. The young of other cervids are probably not because most of them don't have twins and there is a good chance that the mother may have been bred by different bulls in different years. If the same bull elk was dominant and bred the same cow for three years in a row, these calves, even though born in separate years, would be siblings.

Sighting in

All firearms must be sighted in before the gun can be used for either target practice or hunting. Everyone sees iron sights slightly differently, so only the person shooting the gun can do the fine sighting needed. Telescopic sights, having just a single sight pattern, can be sighted for you by a gunsmith or friend if you are not confident of your own ability. After a gun is sighted in, great care must be taken to ensure that the sights have not been knocked out of alignment. All guns that are shipped or carried to a distant hunting camp should be fired to see if the sights are accurate before you actually begin hunting.

(See *Benchrest.*) Bore sighting is a common technique to sight in a new scope-mounted gun. It can only be used with guns in which you can actually look down the barrel. There are also bore-sighting devices that can be used with any gun because they fit in the end of the barrel. No matter what method you use, you should use a benchrest or sandbag to help reduce human error. Use a large background target when you fire your first shots because the sights may be off a foot or more when you start. A spotting scope is a great aid because you will be able to see where your shots are hitting without having to go up to the target. If your shots are grouped tightly, but are not on the bull's eye, the sights need adjustment. If the shots are scattered, it is your fault. Use a more secure benchrest. If you have someone with you, sight again on the bull's eye and, while you hold the sight and gun on the bull's eye, have your friend move the sights to the point of impact and you should be right on target thereafter. (See *Spotting scopes.*)

Sights, laser

The newest innovation in gun sights is the use of a laser beam. The sight is adjusted until the red dot is precisely where you want the point of impact to be. These sights are popular on short-range firearms.

Single-shot rifle

The simplest form of action is the single-shot rifle, which must be reloaded each time the spent casing is ejected. The exception is the muzzleloading rifle, wherein more powder and the ball must be rammed down the barrel to reload. The single-shot rifle may use a break-open, falling block, or bolt action to seat the cartridge.

Single-shot shotgun

As its name implies, this is a single-barreled shotgun that is opened at the breech so the new shell can be inserted and the fired hull ejected. It usually has an exposed hammer. This is the type of shotgun most youngsters start with, which is unfortunate because, being a single barrel, the gun is lighter in weight and the recoil can be punishing in the larger gauges. Single-shots are often viewed as safer for neophytes as they restrict the user to only one shot, as opposed to pumpguns and autoloaders that allow several quick, and often hurried, shots.

Singletons

Mammals giving birth to just one young are said to have a singleton. If they give birth to two young, they are twins, while three young are triplets, four are quadruplets, and five are quintuplets. White-tailed deer, among the Cervidae, are known to have quadruplets and very rarely even quintuplets.

This white-tailed doe has only a singleton. Credit: Len Rue, Jr.

Sitka black-tailed deer (*O. h. sitkensis*)

The Sitka blacktail is an animal of the coastal rainforests of British Columbia and southeastern Alaska. In the winter, food is scarce and deep snows force the deer down to the seashore, where they survive on seaweed and kelp. This sub-species is slightly smaller than the Columbian blacktail. This would seem to be a refutation of Bergmann's Rule, but in this case the size of the deer is more directly connected to diet than to latitude, bringing Rue's Rule into effect.

Sixth sense

A woman's intuition is the best description of a sixth sense at work; it is an internal feeling that something is about to happen when you haven't been warned by sight, smell, hearing, touch, or taste. Yet you know that you know. This sense is much more highly developed in primitive people. It has almost been eradicated in most of us by our way of life. Wildlife all have a more functional sixth sense because their lives are constantly exposed to danger.

Sixth tine

The sixth extension on the main beam is called the sixth tine, or G-6, in deer and elk.

Skewed sex ratio

A skewed sex ratio is when there are more of one gender than there are of the other. Almost all mammals are born, under normal conditions, with a 50/50 sex ratio. In most areas of North America, from the early 1900s to the 1960s, "bucks only" hunting laws were in effect. Everything was done to protect the does as the deer populations were struggling to recover after their near extirpation in most areas. It was not uncommon for the sex ratio to be skewed as much as seven to eight adult does to one adult buck. Whitetails also have an internal population control. When the deer population has grown so large that the habitat is destroyed and starvation is rampant, the does that do produce fawns produce more buck fawns than they do doe fawns, skewing the ratio in favor of bucks, which cuts back on population expansion and gives the range a chance to recover.

Ski hoof

Occasionally, members of the deer family do not walk on the tips of their toes as they should. The hooves of all of these animals are like our fingernails; they grow constantly. When the tips of the hooves do not get the proper wear to keep them worn down, they grow up and become very elongated, causing the ski tip appearance. Deer living in swampy areas always have longer tips than do those that live on rocky ground. The sitatunga antelope of Africa spends its entire life in swamps, and the elongated hoof is normal for them.

The ski hooves of an old white-tailed buck. Credit: Marilyn Maring

Skinning

Skinning your animal should not be done until you are ready to butcher the animal. This will protect the exterior meat from drying out and being lost. I fully realize that moose and elk often have to be skinned at once so the meat can be cut apart to be moved. Most hunters hang their deer up by their hind legs using a gambrel and skin the animal from the hind legs down toward the cape. This is best if you are going to cape out a trophy for mounting. I prefer to hang the deer by the head because the carcass drains free of all blood better. Then I skin from the head toward the hind legs. Deer are skinned open because the belly skin has already been cut in order to eviscerate the animal when it was shot. As soon as I hang my deer, I put a 10-inch stick in the chest cavity to spread the ribs to allow the carcass to cool more quickly from the inside.

Sleep

Most wild animals sleep in extremely short snatches of perhaps thirty seconds or less. Eternal vigilance is the price of life. They must constantly be alert to possible danger from a predator or hunter. Most cervids sleep with their heads held up and can sleep with their eyes wide open or just half-open. Only if they feel secure do their eyes close momentarily. Their ears never stop moving. Some sleep standing up, although the majority lie down. Only when the animals are completely exhausted or feel exceptionally secure do they rest with their heads upon the ground.

Slugs

In an effort to make shotguns more effective at longer ranges, the ammunition companies have developed new and different types of slugs. (See *Rifled slugs.*) Some companies are putting rifling in the barrels, which allows the slug to spin, allowing for shots out to 100 yards. Probably the most accurate types of slugs are the sabots, first used in Europe. These slugs have an hourglass-shaped design and, when used in the rifled shotgun, offer the greatest accuracy.

Snort

All deer snort when frightened, although does are more likely to snort than bucks; they are just more suspicious of potential danger. Deer snort by forcing air from the lungs up through the nostrils with the mouth closed. Snorting is just an attention-getting warning. It is given when the deer suspects danger but has no proof of it. The snort is usually accompanied by a stomping of the feet and a flaring of the tail and rump hair. All deer pay attention to a snort and foot stomping, but they seldom run off because they don't know if the danger is real or where it might be. When a deer can confirm danger with its nose or eyes, it gives a snort-wheeze. This is a much louder, higher-pitched snort, given with the mouth open. The snort-wheeze is never challenged; *all* deer explode into action in all directions, even if they have not detected the danger themselves. The snort-wheeze literally blows all the deer out of the area.

Snow insulation

I have always said that deer were a southern species that is working its way north all the time, in part due to global warming. I based this observation on the fact that deer do not utilize snow properly to get the greatest insulative quality from it. Biologists have just proven that deer are a southern species moving north. Northern animals, such as moose and caribou, always lie down in undisturbed snow if possible so that the snow envelopes their bodies. Snow is actually 80 percent dead air, and dead air provides excellent insulation. Deer do not take advantage of this. Deer always paw a bed before lying down, and this does not allow the snow to wrap around their bodies. Although the insulative quality of their winter hair prevents the loss of most body heat, the enveloping snow would save them many additional calories.

White-tailed doe pawing a bed in snow.

Social carrying capacity

Whereas the carrying capacity of the land denotes how many animals can live there without destroying the habitat, the social carrying capacity is a new term denoting how many animals the people who own that land will tolerate. Game departments all over the country have become increasingly aware that their management plans must take into consideration all of the factors involving wildlife, not just efforts to maximize huntable populations. It is to reduce deer/car accidents and to prevent destruction of ornamental shrubs and gardens that many states are deliberately reducing their deer herds. While many hunters don't approve of such reductions, almost all of them understand the necessity of doing so.

Social grooming

Social grooming is a bonding action between a doe and her fawn, between siblings, between adult does in their maternal groups, and among adult bucks in their fraternal groups. The mutual licking, which is usually done around the head area and often done simultaneously, deposits each participant's saliva on the other, strengthening familial and social ties. Bucks often lick each other's glandular head scents. Sometimes they remove ticks from each other because the head and neck area is the only area on their own bodies that deer can't reach. The grooming may start with a subordinate animal licking a dominant animal, but the licking is most often mutual. It's a case of "you scratch my back and I'll scratch yours."

Socioeconomic factors

In most of the rural communities of the United States, hunting is not only a basic part of the fabric of people's everyday life, it is also the basis for their economic survival.

Sodium

A metallic element occurring naturally in salt and other compounds. It is found, and used, in many different forms. It is essential to all living creatures.

Sound shots

Do not take sound shots. Never shoot at something you can't positively identify as being a proper target. Too many hunters have been shot by other hunters who fired indiscriminately at sounds they heard in the woods without confirming that they had a clear shot at a game animal.

Southern mule deer (*O. h. fuliginatus*)

This subspecies is found along California's coast from the vicinity of Los Angeles south into Mexico's Baja California Peninsula. It is a very dark subspecies of about the same size as the California mule deer.

Sparring

Many hunters mistake sparring for fighting. There is a big difference. Sparring is testing, playing, and strengthening and is engaged in by all of the males of all of the cervids. Even at a distance, you can tell if the animals are sparring or fighting by looking at the position of the animals' legs. Because the males are not putting all of their efforts into sparring, the legs are usually straight up beneath their body. In fighting, the legs are spraddled wide and angled sharply back as the animals use all of their efforts to push their opponent backward and to prevent being pushed backward themselves. Fights are usually very intense and only last

A big white-tailed buck sparring with two young bucks.

five to 10 seconds. Sparring often goes on for a half-hour. Any male that ever hopes to breed has to engage in sparring, because dominance is also being determined. So long as the young males don't approach a bigger, older male with an aggressive posture, the older male usually tolerates pushing and sparring with the younger animals. Occasionally sparring turns into a fight between equal animals if one inadvertently hurts the other.

Spicules

Spicules are the little pinprick tips that you can feel when you run your finger over the convex base of a cast antler. When a cervid's antlers are to be cast, a layer of cells beneath the coronet, called osteoclasts, begins to reabsorb calcium from the antlers. The solid mass of the antler becomes grainy until only chambered spicules remain. Eventually just the weight of the antlers is sufficient to cause the remaining spicules to break, and the antler drops off at the pedicel. The roughness at the base of the cast antler is caused by erosion of the spicules.

Spike

Any unbranched antler, no matter its length or the age of the animal, growing from the pedicel is known as a spike. In deer, the growth of spikes is only very rarely a genetic characteristic; it usually results from the lack of a nutritious diet. Formerly, many hunters believed that all deer had spikes as their first set of antlers. Not true. No deer should ever have spikes, and most never will, if they have access to a diet of 16-percent protein.

Splaying

Splaying means spreading out. Sometimes when walking on ice, deer slip, and in falling their legs splay out, dislocating

A white-tailed buck with exceptionally long spikes.

the hind legs at the hip joints and tearing the muscles at the shoulder. Deer with splayed legs do not recover.

Spongiosa

When an antler is growing, it is nourished through the velvet on the outside of the antler as well as the spongiosa on the inside. Spongiosa is the soft inner core of a buck's antlers, composed of bone matrix. Around the first of August, the blood supply to the spongiosa is cut off and it begins to dry, starting at the base. The drying spongiosa has a honeycomb texture. The antlers continue to dry until the antlers drop off. During October and November, when most fights occur, the spongiosa still has moisture in it, which provides resiliency and prevents the antlers from breaking. The drier the spongiosa becomes as the season advances, the more antler breaking increases.

Sport-Wash

Sport-Wash is a cleaning solution for washing camouflage clothing. It has no UV brighteners, which are found in most other washing detergents. The UV brighteners may get your white clothes "whiter than white," but they also allow the deer to see the UV radiation that such detergents put in your hunting clothing. Deer can see in the ultraviolet range of the spectrum—don't use regular washing detergent. You can get Sport-Wash at most sporting goods stores or by contacting Atsko, Inc., 2664 Russell Street, Orangeburg, SC 29115; telephone 803-531-1820.

Spotlight

A spotlight can be a large flashlight, a battery-powered spotlight, or a spotlight fastened to your vehicle. With the new halogen light elements, many of these units will throw a beam of light for a quarter of a mile. They are very useful for seeing deer at night.

CAUTION! Because poachers usually use these lights to see the animals they are taking illegally, many states have strict laws concerning their use. Some restrict the season in which spotlights may be used. Some states have set times after which the lights may not be used, while some states don't allow spotting of wildlife at any time.

Spotting scopes

Spotting scopes are usually monoculars that are much more powerful than binoculars. They range up to 20X, 40X, and even 60X magnification. They must be used on some sort of base, such as a miniature tripod, because they cannot be held steady by hand. They are a must for hunting elk in the mountains and caribou on the tundra. It is much easier to check for potential trophy animals by "glassing" them than it is to clamber over miles of terrain. Spotting scopes are also a great help when you are sighting in your rifle because you can easily see where your bullet is hitting the target at 100 yards without having to walk up to the target each time you shoot. See *Sighting in.*

Squatting

To squat is to bend the hind legs to lower the body close to the ground. All of the cervids squat slightly to urinate. The mule deer squats down so low that the buck's tail almost touches the ground.

Bow hunters often talk of missing a deer because it squatted when they released their arrows, thus causing them to shoot over the deer's back. Deer do not squat to duck beneath the arrow. A snake that is stretched out straight can't strike; it has to coil first. A deer can't jump until it bunches its mus-

A black-tailed doe squatting to urinate.

cles, and to do that, it squats. It's the same principle that requires a bow to be bent to propel the arrow. The flexing has to take place first in order to get action.

Stag

The male cervids on the North American continent are referred to as bucks and bulls. The male European cervids are referred to as stags.

Stalking

The most difficult of all modes of hunting for whitetails is stalking. Because whitetails live in such heavy cover, the hunter cannot see a great distance. As the whitetails are usually bedded and not moving while the hunter is moving, *all* of the advantages are with the deer. Stalking cannot be done when the leaves are crisp and dry; even the most careful hunter sounds like he is walking on cornflakes. Rainy days or a wet snow are best because wet leaves make no noise. Great care must be taken to hunt into the wind. The hunter must use 90 percent of his time scrutinizing every piece of terrain and 10 percent moving forward after the scrutiny. Very few hunters can successfully stalk whitetails.

Stalking is much more common for elk, caribou, and moose. Except for moose in the northeastern forests, most of the terrain out west and up north is open montane or open tundra where the animals can be seen for long distances. In these places, the animal hearing one move is not so much of a problem; the hunter just has to stay out of sight and downwind.

Standers

In making deer drives, the drivers attempt to push the deer past the standers. It is extremely important that the drivers know where the standers will be. Standers must be absolutely sure that none of the drivers are in line with any game that they shoot at. This is one reason why shotguns are the favored weapon for deer drives—they don't shoot as far. Standers should be placed on known deer travel and escape routes and usually are assigned such spots by the hunt coordinator. See *Deer drive.*

Starvation

It has been biologically proven that if a deer goes into the winter period of lowered metabolism with an ample supply of fat on and in the body, it can go 65 days without eating and still survive. It is also a biological fact that when a deer loses 33 percent of its total body weight, it is going to die of starvation. A deer that has lost a third of its body weight has used up all of its fat reserves, including the fat in the marrow of its bone. The deer is greatly weakened because even some of its muscles have been catabolized for energy needed to live. Fawns, having fewer body reserves than do adult deer, die in greater numbers during periods of starvation. When severe winters are forecast,

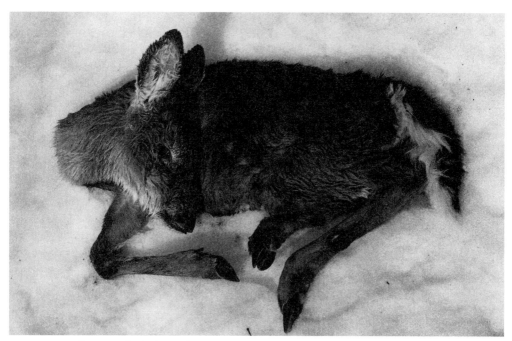

A young white-tailed deer dead of starvation.

hunters should shoot the six- to seven-month-old fawns, where legal, because they will be the first to die from starvation.

State game land

These are areas where the state has purchased land, usually with money from the sale of hunting licenses, that is open to hunting and to the general public for recreation. Forests are often managed, food plots are planted, and wetlands are created and maintained to benefit all kinds of wildlife. Pennsylvania has done an outstanding job, having thousands upon thousands of acres put aside for recreation. These lands will never be developed.

Sterilants

A number of state game departments have been experimenting with sterilants in order to lower the population of white-tailed deer in urban areas where they can't be hunted. Some communities, such as Fire Island, New York, hire private companies to administer the sterilants. On Fire Island, the control officers use blowguns to propel the syringes. In every case, sterilants are not cost-effective because there are no long-term medications. Most medications must be administered at least once a year. Even where dart guns can be used, the control officer still has to be fairly close to the deer in order to hit it with the drug. When even the most controlled public hunting cannot be allowed, communities are now turning to companies that provide skilled certified marksmen.

Stiffen up

A hotly debated question is whether to follow a deer as soon as it is shot or wait 20 minutes or so for the deer to lie down and "stiffen up." A wounded deer does not stiffen up until it dies and rigor mortis sets in; that stiffens them up. According to the temperature, a deer usually becomes "stiff" about one hour after dying.

I always recommend that a wounded deer be followed at once to keep the blood flowing. A wounded deer that is allowed to lie down will have time for its blood to coagulate so that it no longer bleeds or leaves a blood trail. It is important to get enough blood out of the deer to cause death.

Still-hunting

See *Stalking.*

Stocks

The stocks on firearms are made from many different materials. The early Kentucky rifles (made in Pennsylvania) favored curly maple stocks because of the beautiful grain in the wood. Most modern firearms have stocks made of walnut, which is a very strong wood with a tight grain that allows for good checkering design. The finer pieces of walnut also have beautiful grain patterns. Today, some of the newest rifles have hard plastic or composite stocks that are very practical, if not as beautiful as wood. The plastic and composite stocks are virtually indestructible. Wooden stocks can be broken, are easily scratched and dented, and may warp if used in days of rain. The warping can put pressure on the barrel and change the gun's point of impact. Some wooden stocks have a fiberglass bedding to prevent warping. To "feel" absolutely right, a stock must "fit" the person shooting the gun. That is why custom-made guns feel better, because the fit is better. As we are all different in body size, some of us need larger stocks, some need higher combs on the gun, some need more drop to the stock, some prefer a pistol grip to a straight stock, and on and on. Your gun is only as good as its stock.

Stotting

Stotting is a gait employed by both mule deer and black-tailed deer. It is a bouncing, bounding gait wherein all of the deer's four feet leave the ground at the same time, as if it were using a pogo stick. It is an adaptation that allows the animal to negotiate steep ground very quickly. For climbing steep mountainsides, stotting is much more energy-efficient than the galloping gait of whitetails.

The offspring of crossbreeding between white-tailed bucks and mule deer does are not as efficient in either stotting or galloping as either of respective parents, and are thus more easily taken by predators.

Stress

Pressure brought on by exposure to outside circumstances. All of the cervids are stressed very easily by heat, so during the summer they lie in cool places and wait until the sun starts to wane. All of the cervids have a good start on their winter coats in September, and if the day is warm, they will not move. If they are frightened by a predator, the adrenaline pumping through their system causes stress. The competition and the chasing and fighting during the rutting season also cause stress. The most

White-tailed buck stressed by running.

commonly seen symptom of stress is when the animal stands with its mouth open, gulping air rapidly.

Submissive posture

Body language is one of the most important means of communication among mammals. Each creature is very aware of the messages it is sending and also the messages it is receiving. Eye aversion is the most important pacifier used to defuse or neutralize aggression. Even the most dominant, aggressive buck will allow a lesser buck to approach so long as the lesser buck does so in the submissive posture of holding his head down and having his ears pointing forward. The lesser buck may even touch noses with the dominant buck and smell his forehead scent glands before stepping back. When no aggressive signals are given, no aggressive response is needed.

Subordinate

Every creature would like to be number one, including you and me. However, there can be only one number one. Number two

Although the yearling bull moose is definitely subordinate, it is playfully challenging a two-year-old bull moose to spar.

is subordinate to number one, but dominant over number three and all others in the hierarchy below. Number three is subordinate to both number one and number two, but dominant over all others, and so it goes to the most inferior creature in the lineup.

Subsistence harvests

In many areas of North America, the native-born people are not subject to the same game laws that govern the rest of us. This is mainly because many of the native people depend upon wildlife for subsistence, for the food needed for their very survival. For many native people, these subsistence rights go back to the treaties made with the government that took their land. Such treaties usually said that "so long as the grass grows and the rivers flow," they can hunt, trap, and fish forever.

Subspecies

A species is a scientific classification of similar-appearing creatures that are capable of breeding and bearing young. For example, the white-tailed deer is classified with the Greek word *Odocoileus,* meaning "hollow tooth," with *virginianus* as the prototype because the species was first seen in the state of Virginia. All of the whitetails in North America thus have *Odocoileus virginianus* as the species type, but the third name, *borealis,* is their subspecies classification, based on slight differences from other subspecies. Each subspecies, and there are 17 whitetail subspecies north of the Mexican border, also has its home range area.

Succulent forage

Succulent refers to vegetation having a high water content. All vegetation is most succulent in the spring when the plants are putting forth new growth. Most plants dry as they mature and then die. Different types of plants have different cell structures, and some have cells containing much more liquid at all times than other plants. The legumes, such as alfalfa, trefoil, and sweet peas, have much more moisture than do the grasses, such as timothy and orchard grass.

Sudoriferous glands

Sudoriferous glands are scent-producing glands. They are the glands found beneath the skin on the deer's forehead. Both males and females have them, although the males have many more of them. The glands are quiescent in the summertime, but increase greatly in size and production of glandular secretions before and during the rutting season. The more dominant the buck is, the more active his glands will be. The dominant buck will always have the darkest skullcap, stained by his forehead secretions.

Summer coat

The whitetail, blacktail and mule deer have two annual periods of molting per year. The summer coat is worn in May, June, July, and August and changes in September. In the case of the whitetail, the summer coat is a bright russet-red in color. The summer coat has hair that is thin, short, and solid, with about 5,200 hairs to the square inch. The coat is designed primarily for protection from insects and heat reflection. There is no woolly undercoat between the summer hairs.

Sunrise and sunset

It is critical that you know the exact timing of sunrise and sunset in your area, because the legal hunting hours in most areas are from precisely ½ hour before sunrise to only ½ hour after sunset.

Sustainability

This term is usually used in conjunction with habitat. Only good habitat can sustain a good population of any creature, particularly the cervids. The goal of almost all wildlife management programs a few years ago was to increase the amount of food available in a given area in order to produce the largest number of huntable species. They tried to maintain, to sustain, huntable wildlife at its highest peak.

Sweat glands

Biologists claim that deer do not have sweat glands, and I can't prove that they do. However, I have many photographs of white-tailed bucks that are soaking wet from exertion during the peak of the rutting season. I have not seen deer "lathered" with sweat as horses sometimes are, but their coats become so wet that the hairs separate into ridges and rows.

Although biologists claim that deer do not have sweat glands, this white-tailed buck was "sweat-wet" from exertion.

Swimming ability

All of the cervids are excellent swimmers, with the caribou perhaps the best. Because of their hollow, air-filled winter hair, all cervids are actually buoyed up by their coats. Caribou swim with their bodies higher in the water than any of the other cervids. In the fall, the soft portion of the caribou's hooves shrink, making their feet much more effective paddles. Whitetails have been known to swim 12 to 15 miles to islands they can't even see but know are there by scent.

White-tailed deer are strong swimmers.

Symbiosis

Symbiosis is when two different creatures both benefit from the actions of one another. In Yellowstone National Park, I have often seen cowbirds ride on the backs of elk, picking off ticks and flies. The cowbirds get food and the elk get relief. That's symbiosis.

τ

Tagging

As a photographer, I hate to see animals carrying radio collars or wearing ear tags. As a naturalist, I fully realize that it is only by being able to positively identify an individual animal that we can study its range, life span, activity, and so on. Our knowledge of wildlife exploded after tagging programs were undertaken.

Taiga

A Russian word, meaning "land of little sticks." A taiga is a transition area between the northern boreal forests and the treeless tundra. It is characterized by the spindly, shortened black spruce trees.

Taiga moose

This is another name for the eastern moose *Alces alces americana.*

Tails

The tail of the mule deer is pendant-shaped, with white hairs all around it and a black tip. It cannot be confused with

Left to right: the tails of white-tailed, mule, and black-tailed deer.

the tail of any of the other deer. The black-tailed deer's tail has a black upper surface with a white underside; however, the hairs are short, and the tail cannot be flared or raised up over the animal's back. The whitetail's tail is usually brown on the upper surface and bright white on its undersurface. The hairs are long, and the tail can be flared about 10 inches wide. The whitetail, in running, often raises its tail absolutely vertical. Occasionally, the upper surface of the whitetail's tail will be ¼, ½, ¾, or totally black. This is a genetic condition and not the result of crossbreeding with the black-tailed deer.

Tannic acid

Tannic acid is a compound found in many different types of vegetation. It is found in small amounts in the tea we drink, giving the tea its brown color. It is found in large amounts in the rotting vegetation found in swamps, giving the water its "cedar" color. It is found in the bark and wood of oaks, chestnuts, and other trees and is used for commercial tanning of leather. It is found in varying degrees in acorns. White oak acorns have the least amount of tannic acid, which is why deer prefer them over all other acorns. Chestnut oak acorns are bitter with tannic acid, and deer eat them only if food is scarce.

Tanning

Tanning is the process of treating an animal's hide so that it does not stiffen or spoil and so it can be used as leather. The Indians usually tanned animal skins, after the hair had been removed, with the animal's brain and sometimes with a bit of the liver. Each animal's brain is large enough to provide the ingredients to tan its own hide. The hides were then twisted repeatedly to break the fibers and smoked to keep them soft. The Eskimos frequently tanned their hides with urine. Commercial tanning is done with tannic acid and other chemicals.

Tapetum lucidum

A reflective surface behind the retina in an animal's eye that bounces the light back through the rods and the cones, effectively doubling the available light. Creatures having the tapetum can see much better in the dark. It is the tapetum that causes the "eye shine" that people see when light is shone on the eyes of a deer, cat, raccoon, or other such animal.

Tarsal gland

The tarsal gland is located on the inside of a deer's foot at the juncture of the tibia, or main leg bone, and the tarsus, corresponding to our ankle. Beneath the skin are subaceous and sudoriferous glands connected to hair follicles that are ducts bringing the secretions to the long tufts of hair. The secretions have no odor, but they do have lipids that hold the urine deposited on the hairs by the deer. Bacterial action on the lipids and urine produces the strong musky odor for which this gland is noted. All deer urinate on their tarsal glands from time to time. Fawns begin to urinate on their tarsal glands as early as one week of age. The more dominant

Notice how dark the tarsal glands are on this dominant buck.

the buck, the more frequently he urinates on these glands and the darker the hair around the gland will be.

Taxidermy

Taxidermy is the careful preservation of wildlife skins in as lifelike a position and condition as is possible. Most creatures are mounted today on pre-cut forms that are anatomically correct to the finest detail. Taxidermy is really an art form today, as the creatures look so real you expect them to move. While most taxidermy is still done with skinning, tanning, and sewing procedures, many of the smaller creatures are preserved by freeze-drying. Most states require taxidermists to be licensed, and they must pass rigorous tests before receiving their license.

Taxonomy

This is the scientific classification of all living creatures. For example, the white-tailed deer of Minnesota is classified as follows:

Kingdom Animal (animals, birds, fishes, etc.)
Phylum   Chordata (having a backbone)
Class   Mammalia (having mammary glands)
Order   Artiodactyla (meaning even-toed, as the deer has 4 toes on each foot)
Family   Cervidae (deer, elk, caribou, moose)
Genus   Odocoileus (the whitetail is *Odocoileus virginianus,* the mulie is *Odocoileus hemionus*)
Species *Virginianus borealis* (specifically designates the northern woodland whitetail)

Originally creatures were classified because of physical similarities. Today DNA is proving relationships not visible to the naked eye, helping taxonomists to more properly classify creatures.

Teeth

Basically, most mammals are assigned to their family group based on the type of teeth they have. All rodents have just two incisor teeth in the front of their mouths in both the top and bottom jaws. If they don't have those four teeth, they are not rodents. Rabbits, hares, and pikas used to be classified as rodents, but it was discovered they had two additional little, useless teeth behind the two incisors in the front of their top jaws. Thus, these animals are now re-classified as lago-morphs. None of the cervids have any teeth in the front of their top jaws; the bottom incisor teeth clip off vegetation against a pad of gristle. We humans have 32 teeth; all of the cervids have just 30 teeth.

Tendon click

When caribou walk, they make an audible clicking sound. The clicks are made when the animal puts its weight on the hoof and the tendons slip over the tarsal bones above the hooves. It is thought that the clicking sound enables the herd to stay together when they migrate on dark nights.

Territory

A true territory is an area claimed by a male and female from which they attempt to drive out all members of the same species. A territory is needed for some creatures to be assured that they have an area large enough to provide food for themselves and their families. Some creatures, such as wolves, may have several generations included in their pack, and all of the related members help the dominant pair defend the territory. None of the cervids have territories, except for the white-tailed doe's short-term "birthing territory," from which she will drive all other deer, including her last year's fawns. The cervids have home ranges; they may have summer and winter ranges.

Testosterone

The basic male hormone that makes a male a male. Testosterone is a steroid androgen produced in the male's testicles. Carried throughout the body by the bloodstream, it is the switch that turns on or off the bucks' yearly cycle of activity.

Texas white-tailed deer (*O. v. texanus*)

This subspecies is found in western Texas, Oklahoma, Kansas, southeastern California, eastern New Mexico, and the northern portion of Mexico. Its body is smaller than the northern subspecies, which makes Texas bucks' antlers look even larger in comparison. They do produce some world-record bucks.

A Texas white-tailed buck.

Thermals

Thermals are currents of air created by the lowering or rising of the ambient temperature. In the morning, as the sun warms the earth, thermals rise because warm air is lighter than cold air. In hilly or mountainous country, thermals may not rise straight up, but instead flow uphill at ground level. In the evening, as the sun wanes, or sets, the earth cools off and the thermals flow down the hill. It is for this reason that deer like to bed up near the top of the ridges. As the day warms up, the scent of everything below them is wafted up to the bedded deer. This is why hunters will have a better chance of harvesting their deer by getting up on the ridges early, above the deer, and walking the ridges, watching carefully down each side.

Thermoregulation

Any physical property that helps to change a creature's body temperature is a thermoregulator. Most deer have almost no hair on their ears in the summertime. This allows the blood flowing through the ears to cool before being returned to the body. The velvet on a buck's growing antlers helps to dissipate its body heat in the same fashion. All cervids pant during hot weather, and this gets the warm internal heat from the lungs out of the body faster. The hairy covering on the wide muzzles of moose and caribou helps to prevent the loss of body heat. The long, hollow, winter hair, combined with the woolly underfur, helps the cervids retain their body heat. The loss of their body heat is so low that snow will not melt off their backs.

The extra-large ears on the mule deer help in thermoregulation.

Ticks

Any of the different species of arachnids, such as the deer tick, dog tick, Lone Star tick, or wood tick. All of the ticks are parasites, biting through the skin and drinking the blood of animals, birds, and reptiles. In small numbers, ticks are nuisances. In large numbers, they may weaken the host creature and may even cause its death directly or by allowing infection through the breaks in the skin made by the ticks. The deer tick may cause Lyme disease in humans. The Lone Star tick can be devastating to fawns. Rocky Mountain spotted fever may also be transmitted to humans by ticks.

Tipi-ing

Quite often, cervids browse some shrubs so severely that the shrubs take on a tapered appearance, like that of a Christmas tree or an Indian's tipi.

A live oak overbrowsed by black-tailed deer, giving it a tipi appearance.

Topo map

Topographic maps are available for almost every spot of land in North America. Produced by the U.S. Geological Survey, they accurately portray the ups and downs of the terrain. Every feature of the altitude of the land is noted, as is every physical property. The maps are usually designed with the altitude laid out in 20-foot gradients as contour lines. Every map is laid out with north shown at the top of the map, east to the right, west to the left, and south at the bottom.

Every map shows the difference in declination between the magnetic north, to which your compass will point, and true north, depicted on the map. No one should venture into a wilderness area without a topo map and a compass—and the knowledge of how to use both. Topo maps are a great aid in hunting as they show the gaps in mountain ridges that game animals will follow. They also show stream direction. Topo maps are also used with the GPS system.

Tower blinds

Tower blinds are enclosed blinds that are raised up 15 to 20 feet above the ground. Most of them are built as stationary blinds, but there are commercial ones available that can be moved from one location to another. An advantage to the blinds being permanent is that the deer see them every day and soon accept their presence as a part of the natural landscape. Tower blinds are much more commonly used in the southern states. Almost all hunting done on shooting preserves, all over the country, is done from tower blinds.

Track counts

Taking a census of deer by track counts is usually accomplished by counting the number of tracks crossing roads. In warm weather, on dirt roads, a large evergreen tree is dragged behind a truck crosswise to the road. This usually rubs out all of the previous tracks, and the new tracks are counted early the next morning. Roads may also be driven right after a fresh snow, which makes it easy to count the tracks. Track counts work best in the areas of the country, such as in the Midwest, where most of the land is laid out in one square mile blocks.

Tracking

Tracking is a lost art because it is so seldom practiced. Almost no hunter today can track a deer on hard ground or through dry leaves. Most hunters don't have the time or patience to follow the tracks of a deer, even on snow. Those who do become well-known. My friends the Benoit family of Duxbury, Vermont, are probably the most famous trackers in the country. They are famous for getting on the track of a big buck and staying on it until they get him. Most hunters need to know if the track they are looking at in the snow or mud is that of a buck or a doe. You have to take into consideration when the track was made. Tracks that have sharp edges are usually fresh. Rain will soften the edges of tracks made in the mud before the rain. It's impossible to tell the size of a track in fluffy snow because there are no edges. Tracks made in wet snow enlarge each day as they are exposed to the sun. After just one day, most tracks in snow begin to glaze over in the bottom.

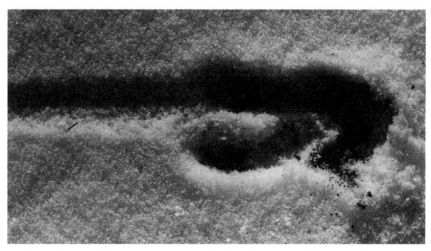

In less than ½ inch of snow, only bucks leave drag marks.

In walking, the track of the deer's hind foot is on top of the track made by the front foot.

The tracks of a running deer are usually splayed apart, making the tracks appear much larger, while those of a walking deer are separated by about ¼ inch. The tracks of a deer's front feet are slightly larger than those of the hind feet. The clear tracks that you see are those of the hind feet, because a walking deer tends to step on the tracks made by its front feet. As a rule of thumb, a track of a deer's hind foot that measures 1¾ inches across will be a buck weighing about 150 pounds. Does seldom get to be that weight. Tracks larger than two inches indicate a potential trophy buck.

Tracking wounded deer

It is seldom that a deer drops in its tracks when shot. *All* deer should be followed. Deer that are shot while running can go hundreds of yards with their hearts shot out because of the adrenaline in their systems. In following a blood trail, tie a ribbon on the last blood spot so you can come back to that spot again if you lose the trail. Wounded deer often go downhill, not to get water but because it is easier for the deer than going uphill. If you have to trail a wounded deer in the evening, use a Coleman gasoline lantern if possible; I don't know why, but the blood will reflect better from the lantern than from a flashlight. We owe it to the game we hunt to find and kill any wounded animal.

Trails

For seventeen summers, I guided canoe trips into the virgin forests of Quebec, Canada. To get from one lake to another, I followed the portage trails taken by the Indians. However, the Indians didn't originate the trails; they followed the trails that had been made by moose.

All animals instinctively lay out their trails on the easiest path, and the easiest grade in going over a hill. Many of our

Deer trails coming off the mountains.

modern highways follow the original trails made by bison crossing the mountains.

Deer know their home range intimately and use trails to get from one area to another. Although a suspicious deer may sneak through thick brush, if it is pushed hard it will usually run on a trail because the trail is usually free of obstructions that would slow it down. In traveling to and from its bedding areas, the deer will follow the trails, a fact that hunters should take advantage of.

Trajectory

It is a basic law of physics that if a bullet is fired from an absolutely level rifle, and a bullet of the same weight, excluding the case, is dropped at precisely the same time from precisely the same place, the two bullets will fall to earth at precisely the same time because the pull of gravity on the two bullets is the same. To get a bullet out to a target at different distances, the gun barrel has to be raised according to the distance, the bullet's weight, its shape, and foot-pounds of pressure. The greater the distance, the more the gun has to be raised. This arc is the trajectory of the bullet.

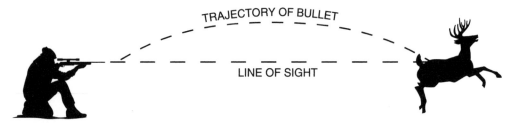

The bullet's trajectory varies above the line of sight according to the distance the hunter is from the target and the speed and shape of the bullet.

Translocation

Translocation means to move from one area to another. Because of the tremendous number of deer that have been moved from one section of the country to another, it is almost impossible to assign the white-tailed deer from any area to a specific subspecies. With almost all sections of the continent having an overpopulation of deer, there is almost no relocation of deer today. Elk are being relocated to many areas, however, and moose are being reintroduced to several.

Transmission of disease

Except when there is an overpopulation of wildlife, there is seldom much transmission of disease. Overpopulation, causing destruction of the habitat, often weakens a species because it is not getting sufficient nutrition to keep its natural immunity high. Overpopulation also concentrates a species, making it easier for the vectors to get from one individual creature to another.

Trauma

Trauma may be caused by an actual physical wound, or it may be caused by stress. Wildlife may be injured by fighting, by a bullet wound, by pursuit of a predator, or by starvation. All or any of these conditions can cause what, in humans, is known as "shock." All of them are detrimental to an animal's survival.

Traveling with guns and ammunition

I know of no restriction on any of the U.S. airlines concerning the transportation of guns and ammunition, provided they are suitably packed and shipped as luggage. It behooves each sportsman to buy the strongest, hard-shell, foam-lined, locking cases available. Airline luggage handlers are not noted for their careful handling of any kind of luggage, and I know of too many horror stories that prove the point. Assume that your gun cases will be thrown about, because they will be.

All transported guns should be fired on a range before they are used for hunting because the rough handling they receive in transit may affect their sight accuracy. The high vibration from the jet engines may also cause screws in scopes to loosen.

Each gun taken into Canada for hunting purposes must be registered at the border with the Canadian government for a one-time fee of $50.

Tree stand

Between 80 and 90 percent of all bow hunters now hunt from tree stands. No one should use a tree stand without using a safety belt. Many accidents occur from hunters falling from tree stands. Tree stands are a very efficient way to hunt for deer because the hunter can usually see the deer coming for a longer distance and thus be ready to take the shot. Most stands are used at 12 to 15 feet above the ground. More important than height is camouflage, so the hunter is not silhouet-

Most bow hunters hunt deer from tree stands.

ted. If you don't have branches behind your stand, you should use a skirt of material around your stand. Most stands can be used as climbing stands; others must be carried up and locked into place. *Don't forget your safety belt.*

Tree steps

If you use a self-climbing stand, you won't need the steps. If yours is not a climbing stand, you must use a ladder, tree spurs, or tree steps in order to climb the tree. Tree steps work very well, as they can be screwed into the tree quite easily and they provide a safe step to climb on. Don't make the space between the steps too far to save having to put in another step or two. When you are done using your stand, you can remove the steps on your way down. If you plan to use the same location again, just remove the bottom three or four steps so that no one else can get up to the other steps. Using tree steps does not permanently injure the tree, as the tree will form new growth in the hole that the screw made.

Trefoil

Trefoil is a member of the legume family, which also includes alfalfa and garden peas. Legumes have the ability to absorb nitrogen from the air and return it to the soil through nodules on their roots. Trefoil, particularly "birdsfoot" trefoil, is recommended as a top planting for deer. It is higher in protein than alfalfa, stands up better to grazing, is longer-lived, reseeds, and spreads itself. It is not as good a hay-producing crop as alfalfa.

Trespassing

In the United States, the wildlife belongs to the states, but most of the land is in private ownership. Landowners have the right to post their land if they want to stop all hunting, reserve hunting rights for personal use, or lease the land to a hunting club. To prevent trespassing, the land must be posted with signs that are intervisable. That means that when you stand by one sign, you can see the next sign on either side of you. To give landowners the protection they need, fines for illegal trespassing have been rising.

Trez tine

The trez tine is the third tine, or point, on the main beam of an elk's, or red deer's, antlers.

A world-record caribou bull, truly a trophy. Credit: Tim Lewis Rue III

Trophy

A trophy is a different thing to different people. It is a term usually used to describe an outstanding animal, an unusually large specimen. The Boone & Crockett Club for gun hunters and the Pope & Young Club for bow hunters are the official registrars of trophy animals of a specified size. An animal that is large enough to be listed in either of their record books is truly a trophy animal, and no one can argue that point. Yet even animals that were not large enough to "make the books" but were an outstanding challenge to take are also truly trophy animals.

Trophy recognition

It is exceedingly difficult to judge the size of a buck's antlers if he is dashing through the woods. However, if you see a buck standing still, you can get a rather accurate estimation of the size of his antlers by remembering that a whitetail's ears are about 7 to 7½ inches long, while a mulie's ears are about 9 inches in length. If the buck is alert and looking at you with his ears flared out, a whitetail will be 16 to 17 inches from ear tip to ear tip, while a mule deer will be 20 to 21 inches. Knowing that, you can estimate the size of the buck's rack by seeing if the ears are larger than the rack or if the antlers extend beyond the ears and by how much. Ear length will also allow you to estimate tine length.

If you see two bucks together and their antlers seem to be about the same size, shoot the buck with the darkest hair on his forehead or skullcap. The more dominant a buck, the more active are his forehead scent glands, and the secretions will stain the hairs darker.

Mature bucks have much deeper bodies, and their chest girth is much larger than 1½- to 2½-year-old bucks. On mature bucks, the neck swelling is always much larger, some reaching a circumference of 40 inches at the shoulder. The hair on the neck of a mature buck separates into vertical layers, or splits, much more apparently than does the hair of younger bucks. Mature bucks walk much more heavily and purposefully than immature bucks do because they are heavier.

Trophy room

A trophy room can be as simple as a living room with several good-sized deer heads or as elaborate as a vaulted-ceilinged room with a lifetime's collection of trophy animals from all over the world. Elaborate trophy rooms cost a lot of money for a number of reasons. It takes a lot of money to hunt all over the continent or the world. It takes a lot of money to have all of the trophies mounted, especially when full-sized body mounts are done. Full-sized mounts take up lots of space, which necessitates a large room, and the larger the room, the more money it costs to build and maintain. Trophy rooms, large or small, are a great source of pride among hunters.

Tuberculosis

Tuberculosis has been found in deer, elk, and moose, but it is a rarity. They are far less susceptible to the disease than are cattle, and when cervids do get it, they usually succumb to the disease rapidly so that it does not get a chance to spread widely.

Tularemia

Tularemia is a disease, caused by the bacteria *Francisella tularensis,* that reaches epidemic proportions in rodents and can be fatal to humans. It is most commonly found in lagomorphs, such as rabbits and hares, or in rodents like muskrats and beaver. Although there have been several cases in both white-tailed and mule deer, these animals are not considered hosts. The disease can be transmitted by tick bites, contaminated water, or contact with infected tissue.

Tule elk (*C. e. nannodes*)

The Tule elk is the smallest subspecies of elk found in the United States, and it has the smallest range. Originally this elk was quite numerous in California, but the land it lived on was good farmland. Today this elk lives in the semi-desert area centered around Kern County, California.

Twinning

Having twins is the norm for healthy adult deer. Young deer usually have singletons during their first pregnancy, but thereafter, if they have access to nutritious food, they usually bear twins until old age. Twins occur occasionally with both elk and moose.

A cow moose and her twin calves.

Two-way radio

Where it is legal to use, a two-way radio set is a great help to hunters—in coordinating deer drives, enabling one hunter to inform a buddy which way game is moving, or helping lost hunters find their way.

u

Udder

The mammary glands or milk bag of all cervids is known as an udder.

Umbilical cord

The umbilical cord is the main lifeline allowing the fetus to develop inside its mother's uterus. The umbilical cord runs from the fetus's abdomen to the walls of the uterus and contains arteries and veins that carry blood and nutrients from the mother to the fetus and carry waste materials back out. The umbilical breaks free during the birth. In most of the cervids, the broken cord, attached to the neonate's navel, is from three to six inches in length. The cord dries rapidly and usually drops off after three days. If you see a dried umbilical cord on an animal, you know that fawn or calf is less than three days old.

Understory

In the process of plant succession, before a forest reaches its climactic stage, there is usually a lot of brushy undergrowth that has not yet been killed by too much shade. This understory provides some of the best foods that deer can eat. When the understory dies out from being denied sunlight by the closed canopy of the mature forest, it is usually replaced by shade-loving ground cover plants such as the ground cedar, princess pine, and ferns of many types. Mushrooms, too, thrive on the decaying vegetation in the deep shade.

Ungulagrades

Bears are plantigrades, as they walk on their entire foot. Cats and dogs are digitigrades because they walk up on their toes. All of the cervids are ungulagrades because they walk up on their toenails.

Ungulates

Ungulates are any of the hoofed mammals. This classification is further split into two groups. The Artiodactyla include all

Bull elk pawing a wallow and urinating.

of the cervids and other creatures having an even number of toes, four in the case of the cervids. The Perissodactyla are odd-toed creatures, with the horse having one visible toe and two buried within the foot, and the rhinoceros having three visible toes.

Urine spraying

Urine is a very important means of communication among most mammals. Deer urinate on their tarsal, or hock, glands, and the urine then drips to the ground in the scrapes. Elk spray urine on their chests and the long hair hanging beneath their necks. They reek of urine and can be smelled at long distances when the wind blows from them to the observer. Both elk and moose make wallows in muddy areas. They tear up the turf with their antlers, paw hollows with their feet, urinate copiously in the hollow, and then lie down and roll in the mud, coating themselves liberally with mud and urine.

Uterus

The female's uterus is the "incubation chamber" in which the fetus develops. During the female's estrus period, a follicle in her ovary ruptures and discharges an egg into the fallopian tube. If the female has been bred, the sperm from the male's semen swims up the fallopian tube. Only one penetrates the egg or eggs which have been discharged. The fertilized egg floats in the uterus as a blastocyst for about nine days. The blastocyst then fastens itself to the wall of the uterus, and the umbilical cord is formed so that nutrients from the mother can nourish the growth of the fetus. The time that the fetus is carried in the uterus is known as the period of gestation. In deer, the gestation period is about 203 days. In elk it is about 253 days, for caribou about 228 days, and for moose it is 243 days. At the end of the gestation period, the fetus is discharged through the cervix, vagina, and out into the outside world.

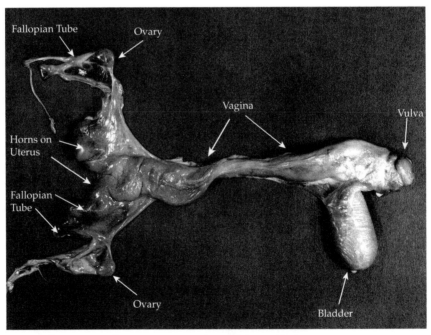

Complete reproductive tract of a whitetail doe.

Vectors

A vector is the agent that transfers disease from one creature to another. Ticks, mosquitoes, flies, and biting midges are the most common vectors. In their need for blood to complete their own life cycle, they ingest blood from infected hosts and transmit the disease to the next creature they parasitize.

Velvet

Velvet is the commonly given name to the network of blood vessels and tissue that forms the outside covering on the growing antlers of cervids. It is the blood vessels that make the longitudinal grooves seen on cast antlers. The hairs on the velvet all stand on end and are a part of the sensory nervous system. Those hairs actually act as a "radar" system that

Huge Alaskan bull moose with dried velvet hanging from his antlers. Credit: Tim Lewis Rue

White-tailed buck's antlers covered with velvet as they start to grow.

warns the deer of obstructions that might injure the growing antlers. The velvet also has sebaceous glands that give off a sebum that acts as an insect repellent. When the velvet dies and dries, it itches, causing the cervid to rub it off. The cervids frequently eat the velvet that they shed.

Vented ports

To reduce the recoil in high-powered rifles, gunsmiths can cut angled slots about two inches from the end of the barrel. These angled slots, or ports, catch part of the gases propelling the bullet out of the barrel and direct them backward, lessening the recoil of the rifle.

Vibrissae

Vibrissae is another word for the long whiskers that cervids have around their muzzles, over their eyes, and under their chins. These long, stiff hairs are attached to sensory nerves that, like a cat's whiskers, act as a "radar screen," informing the animal of precisely how close it is to its physical environment. For example, the vibrissae beneath a deer's chin let it know exactly how close its chin is to the ground when feeding on very dark nights.

The long whiskers and chin hair on this young white-tailed buck are vibrissae.

Viral infections

A viral infection is any one of the many diseases that wildlife is subject to that is caused by viruses that are transmitted by vectors. Some of the most common viral infections are hemorrhagic disease, cutaneous fibromas, and rabies. See *Vectors*.

Virginia white-tailed deer (*O. v. virginianus*)

O. v. virginianus is the prototype for all of the white-tailed deer. It was the first deer of the species to be discovered and named. This is a moderately large deer with fairly heavy antlers. Its range includes Virginia, West Virginia, Kentucky, Tennessee, North Carolina, South Carolina, Georgia, Alabama, and Mississippi. It has a widely diversified habitat ranging

A Virginia white-tailed buck.

from woodlands, coastal marshes, swamplands, and pinelands to the "balds" atop the Great Smoky Mountains.

Viscera

Properly speaking, the viscera is the name for the "guts"—the stomach, intestines, heart, and lungs—of any animal. When you "gut" an animal, you eviscerate it.

Visual advertisement

The rubs and rub lines made by the deer are visual advertisements. The removal of the dark outer bark of trees, which exposes the white inner wood, creates signposts that can be seen for a long distance in the dark woods. Even on the darkest of nights, the white inner wood will reflect whatever minimal light is available.

Vocalization

All of the cervids are far more vocal than most folks realize, because most of the time the sounds they make are not heard by humans, either because of distance or the low tonal range of the sounds. More is known about the vocalization made by whitetails because there are far more whitetails than any other species, they are in closer contact with humans, and they have been more extensively studied. The low-pitched lowing of a white-tailed doe calling its fawn just does not carry far; it's not intended to. The fawn's high-pitched bleat of terror can be heard for a long distance; it's meant to summon help from the doe that is bedded some distance away. The barking call of a cow elk for its nursing calf can be heard for a quarter of a mile. The bugling of a bull elk and the high-pitched lowing of a cow moose can be heard for miles. Cari-

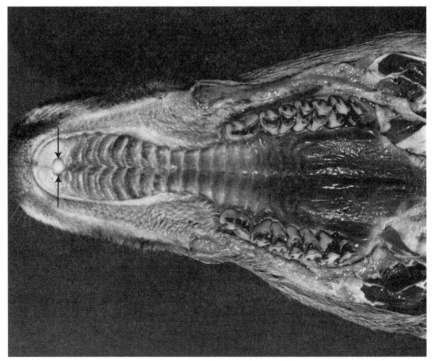

The location of the vomeronasal glands. Credit: Uschi Rue

bou are the most silent of the cervids. The only sound I've heard them make is a low, coughing grunt.

Vomeronasal organ

The vomeronasal organ is located in the top of a cervid's mouth about one inch inside the lip. It corresponds to the Jacobson's organ found in snakes, as it is a means of tracking chemical molecules of scent and changing them into electrical impulses that go to the hypothalmus in the brain, not to the olfactory bulb. It is believed that this organ's job is to prime the buck physically for the doe's estrus period.

Vulva

The external female sexual genitals, including the opening to the internal vagina.

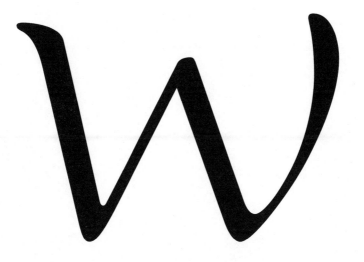

Wallows

Wallows are made by both elk and moose. The males tear up the turf with their antlers in wet areas. They paw the holes deeper with their forefeet. They urinate in the mud and water and then lie down in the mud, coating their bodies with the urine and mud. This is a major means of olfactory communication for these two species.

Wapiti means "white-rumped."

Wapiti

This is the Shawnee Indian name for our North American elk. A literal translation of the word means "white-rumped," referring to the light-colored rump patch that makes the elk so visible when seen from the rear, even at a distance.

Warble fly

Warble flies parasitize most species of wildlife from mice to moose, but they make life hell for the caribou. The adult cutereba fly looks like a large yellow bee. The females lay their eggs on the long hairs of the caribou's legs and are ingested when the animals groom themselves. The eggs hatch and the larvae migrate through the body to skin, usually on the back of the animal. There the larvae cut a hole through the skin to get air and continue their development by feeding on the blood of their hosts. It takes about seven weeks for the larvae to become about one inch in length, at which time they cut through the skin and fall to the ground, where they overwinter beneath the soil to emerge as adult flies in the spring. Heavy infestations of warble larvae create a tremendous drain on the caribou. I have seen caribou skins with over 400 warble scars on them. All of the warbles do not occur at once, but many caribou are infested with as many as 100 warbles each year. As a boy on our farm, I used to pop the warbles out of the skin on the backs of our cows. I could then treat the openings with medication. Fortunately, infection seldom accompanies the exit of the warbles in wild animals.

Wariness

Wariness is an innate trait of almost all wild creatures. Because predation is so high, only the most alert creatures survive. This is survival of the fittest. Where wild animals become accustomed to people, the young are still wary until they, too, become acclimated.

Water

Most creatures can only go about three minutes without air, three days without water, and up to thirty days without food. In the spring and early winter, when dew is common and the vegetation succulent, most of the cervids get their moisture from the vegetation that they eat. As the vegetation matures, it dries; then the creatures must drink free water. A deer needs two to three quarts of water at least twice a day. Elk need several gallons. Moose feeding in water get most of their water, in spring, summer, and fall, from the vegetation

A black-tailed doe and fawn drinking at a spring.

and water at the same time. In the winter, all cervids eat snow or lick ice.

Waterproofing

It's a known fact that you can't be comfortable if your feet are wet. If your feet are wet, they will also be cold if the weather is cold. Despite the claims of the various manufacturers, I still find it best to waterproof my leather boots with one of the many products available. I often spray my boots with silicone. I have used mink oil and pine tar, both of which are good. My favorite is Sno-Seal, which has beeswax as its base. To make the leather more absorbent, I warm the boots first by setting them in the hot sun or near a stove. I also warm the product being used and put the boots back out in the sun or near the stove to allow the material to penetrate. If you cannot find Sno-Seal at your sporting goods store, you can contact the manufacturer, Atsko, Inc., at 2664 Russell Street, Orangeburg, SC 29115; telephone 803-531-1820.

Weaning

Most of the cervids start to wean their young at about two months of age, at which time the young are fully functional ruminants, capable of surviving on just vegetation. Weaning is usually complete at four months of age because the females have to start accumulating fat in their bodies if they are to survive the winter. Some tolerant females will allow their young to nurse briefly up to six months of age. I videotaped a spike bull elk, at 18 months of age, still nursing.

Most white-tailed does allow their fawns to nurse until they are four months old.

Web of life

All things in life are connected. As mentioned in the *balance of nature* entry, what affects one species of plant or animal life will have repercussions somewhere else, even if we are not aware of the connectedness. John Donne once wrote, "No man is an island." Neither is any other living creature. What affects one, affects all, in some fashion, somehow, sometime.

Wild turkeys

Deer do not like to be in an area where wild turkeys are feeding. The turkeys' almost constant scratching makes it exceedingly difficult for the deer to hear any danger that might be approaching. I don't say that deer and turkeys will not feed in the same woodlands at the same time, because they will. I *am* saying that deer don't like to be near wild turkeys when the birds are scratching for food.

Wildlife management

Aldo Leopold, of the University of Wisconsin at Madison, is generally credited with being the father of modern wildlife management. I believe he taught the first courses on the subject. The Indians were the first wildlife managers on this continent when they set fire to the virgin forests to produce brushy growth to increase the deer population. A number of colonies, and then states, wanted conservation laws and set seasons and bag limits on different types of wildlife in order to increase their numbers. Today, wildlife management is being taught in many colleges, and there are thousands upon thousands of professional wildlife managers.

Wind

All hunters must constantly be aware of the direction of the wind, because most wildlife certainly is. Scent is the most important sense of all of the cervids, and if they smell you, they are gone. Wary, suspicious animals will keep out of range and circle until they get downwind of anything that arouses their suspicions.

Most healthy adult animals can withstand extremely cold weather, but they cannot withstand cold weather and wind. The wind blows the cold through their hair, and they rapidly lose body heat.

Winter coat

All of the cervids have long, dense coats of hollow winter guard hairs that provide excellent insulation. They also all have a dense woolly undercoat that provides additional warmth. The whitetail's guard hairs number about 2,600 to the square inch.

These deer are in their heavy winter coats.

Winter feeding

Winter feeding should be undertaken only as the last resort. Most cervids can withstand the cold of winter if they have sufficient nourishment, and they will have sufficient nourishment where they are not overpopulated. To feed deer that are starving because of overpopulation exacerbates the problem because then more deer will survive and the habitat will never have the chance to recover. Except in extreme circumstances, don't feed deer; reduce their population by harvesting more of them.

Wolf

The gray wolf is the largest member of the canine family in North America. It goes by the names of timber, tundra, or Arctic wolf, but they are all basically gray wolves. The wolves live in packs of blood-related family members, with only the dominant pair breeding, although all pack members care and provide for the pups. In wilderness areas, the wolf is the major predator on all of the cervids.

The wolf is a major predator of deer.

Woodland caribou (*R. t. caribou*)

The woodland caribou is the caribou of both the taiga and tundra areas of Canada, from the Yukon Territory east to Newfoundland. The Osborne or mountain caribou of Alberta, British Columbia, and Idaho are now re-classified with the woodland group. Recent efforts to reintroduce the caribou to Maine have failed.

Woodland caribou bulls swimming across a river during migration.

Yarding

In the northern part of their range, the whitetails go to low-lying areas, such as cedar swamps, to "yard" up for the winter. The dense vegetation breaks the force of the wind and the canopy holds a lot of the snow aloft, making it easier for the deer to move about. Most of these yards are traditional and have been used for hundreds of years. The main benefit derived from the yards is protection from the elements; most of the food has long since been eaten. The deer make paths throughout the yard as they seek food, and these trails help them to escape from predators. Ordinarily the bucks stay out on the perimeter of the yards while the does and young deer stay in the center. The bucks' large body size permits them to withstand the cold better, and their larger stomachs allow them to handle coarser vegetation with a higher lignin content.

Yearling

An animal that has passed its one-year birthdate but is not yet two years old is known as a yearling.

Yearling bucks would not have spikes if they had sufficient nutritious food.

Z

Zoonosis

Any disease that can be transmitted from an animal or bird to humans, such as rabies, anthrax, Lyme disease, and Rocky Mountain spotted fever.

The L. L. Rue Catalog Available

Our catalog features a selection of the finest photographic and outdoor equipment, accessories, books, and videos available. Of special interest are the Rue Ultimate Blind, which can be completely set up and ready to use in 30 seconds; the Groofwin Pod, which allows you to photograph from your vehicle window with tripod stability; and the Rue professional photo vest. Other items include camera packs, tripods, tripod heads, protective wraps, lens cases, photographers' gloves, camera mounts, shoulder stocks, and many other useful and unique accessories. Our carefully selected line of nature, outdoor, and photographic books include many written by Dr. Rue: *How I Photograph Wildlife and Nature, The Deer of North America, Way of the Whitetail, Whitetails, How to Photograph Animals in the Wild,* and *Cottontail Rabbit,* among others. Videos by Dr. Rue include *Basics of Bird Photography, Advanced Bird Photography, Rutting Whitetails,* and *An Eye on Nature.*

For a free catalog, please contact: Leonard Rue Enterprises, 138 Millbrook Road, Blairstown, NJ 07825; telephone 908-362-6616; fax 908-362-5808.

For purchase and information about Rue videos, go to *www.ruevideo.com.* For purchase and information about Rue books and catalog items, please go to *www.rue.com.*